CATCHING KNIVES

CATCHING KNIVES

A GUIDE TO INVESTING IN
Distressed Commercial Real Estate

JAKE HARRIS

LIONCREST
PUBLISHING

CATCHING KNIVES

A Guide to Investing in Distressed Commercial Real Estate

ISBN 978-1-5445-2061-2 *Hardcover*

978-1-5445-2060-5 *Paperback*

978-1-5445-2059-9 *Ebook*

As a husband and father, it sounds cliché, but it is the truth. I dedicate this to my wife and kids. My wife, Kristi, is the axis on which my world spins around. Her love and support make this book and everything I do possible. I love you, and the best is yet to come.

To my kids, I feel blessed to be your father and guide you on your journey in this world. You help me strive to be a better man than I was yesterday. I am proud of you, I love you, and I will be the loudest one cheering you on from the front row of your lives.

Kiss, hug, high five, and knuckles.

CONTENTS

INTRODUCTION

My career in real estate investing began with dramatic ups and downs, from becoming a millionaire before thirty, to watching helplessly as the portfolio I built became distressed and deep in debt. I sat on the curb in front of a foreclosed property, losing everything: health, time, relationships, and least importantly, money. But with the help of others, I realized that, though painful, it was one of the best times to be investing. There was "blood in the streets." I was scared, but the lessons I learned while hitting rock bottom allowed me to spend the next dozen-plus years investing in distressed real estate.

Today, I'm the founder of a successful private equity real estate firm that invests in commercial and residential properties on a nationwide scale. I've been responsible for hundreds of millions of dollars across thousands of transactions, I have traveled to a new country every year with my family, and I am in the best shape of my adult life because of the freedoms that have been afforded to me because of distressed real estate investing. But my journey started with the simplest transaction of all: someone handed me a book that changed my life forever.

A REAL ESTATE EPIPHANY

Since my teenage years, I knew I wanted to get involved in business and investing. It started with buying peanut butter M&Ms at a discount grocery store at a wholesale price and selling them around my high school for a 400 percent markup. From there, I turned to "flipping" consumer electronics. I would study what price products were selling for on eBay and then buy in bulk from other competing auction websites and sell them individually back on eBay for a profit.

These activities gave me a taste of business, but I didn't know how to make the leap to something bigger—something I could do for the rest of my life. Then, one day during my time in the army, I was lying on my cot when a friend yelled out, "Hey, Sarge! You should read this."

He tossed me a purple-and-yellow book titled *Rich Dad, Poor Dad* by Robert Kiyosaki, and as I read that book, I experienced one of life's light-bulb moments. I had an epiphany.

The book explained how the rich get richer through real estate investing and how anyone can use that same path to gain wealth, even if they're starting from nothing.

"This is the work I want to do," I said to myself. Real estate investing tapped into my skillsets and excited me, but without mentors and with a limiting belief, I told myself it would take many more years until I could do it myself. So I focused on learning as much as I could while working other jobs.

I started bartending at a golf course, which put me in the same space as millionaires and real estate investors. As I hung around their fringe and served these people drinks, I picked up little gems of information. I talked to them, asked them questions, and made my position clear: "I'm twenty-three, and I want to work in real estate. I'm ready to grab the tiger by its tail."

My networking paid off when one of the country club patrons suggested I get into construction. Everything in real estate involves a contractor, so what better way to get immersed in the space? It was exactly the entrance I needed.

I took a job working in commercial construction. I was unqualified and lacked the proper education, so I had to talk my way into the position. Ultimately, it was my willingness to work for free and my belief that I could learn anything that landed me a starting position as an estimator. Mind you, this was before Google and YouTube, so it was an awkward first couple of weeks trying to figure out the job I had talked myself into. But numbers are my thing, and I took to it like a fish to water. I quickly moved up to superintendent and assistant project manager. Like a sponge, I absorbed whatever experience and knowledge I could gather.

Our client was Sam Zell's Equity Office Properties, and I managed the value-add remodel of several mid-rise office buildings. I coordinated hundreds of subcontractors, balancing relationships with city inspectors, leasing agents, architects, property managers, and more. I was making a decent amount of money and learning valuable skills. However, there was a problem. I lived and worked in the Bay Area of California, which meant the real estate there was extremely expensive. It would take me forever to save the money I needed to invest in property.

I continued to work fixing up and remodeling office buildings, but my goal seemed impossible to me, like a mountain too high.

Then an opportunity presented itself. I'd gone to Phoenix, Arizona, to buy some cars at auction for resale. Even though I had a full-time job, I was still working on the side on other deals. While in Phoenix, I happened to have some extra time in town. As I drove through subdivisions of new homes being built, what I saw shocked me. These houses cost only $100,000 to $150,000—at the time, you could not have bought an outhouse for those prices in the Bay Area. The Phoenix home prices were a quarter, or even a tenth, of the price of houses in California. *This market*, I realized, *I can actually afford to invest in.*

BECOMING AN INVESTOR

I was twenty-five when I bought my first house in Glendale, Arizona: a fixer-upper across the street from the Westgate District and the soon-to-be-built Cardinal Stadium. But soon after that purchase, something occurred that made the decision feel very untimely. I was laid off from my job at the construction company. I had planned to fly down to Phoenix on the weekends to fix up the house, but with no job and nothing tying me to California, I decided instead to move into the house and work on it full time. I put a few tools in the back of my truck and headed to Arizona.

Every nickel and dime I had went into buying that house, so when I moved in, I had almost nothing left. I slept on a mattress on the floor that the realtor gave me. I kept my food in a Styrofoam cooler and every couple of days bought new bags of ice because I had no refrigerator. I utilized every last penny to renovate the property, and just before running out of money, barely making it to the finish line, I put it on the market.

The house sold quickly for a $17,000 profit. Wow! I was hooked, and intent on repeating the process, I bought another property and then made $28,000. I bought another one, which netted $35,000. In short order, I was living the process the way I'd imagined years earlier. I became myopically focused on a single goal: to become a millionaire before age thirty. Investing in real estate was the vehicle that would take me there.

Over the next several years, the market thrived. This was the run-up of the subprime bubble, and capital flowed in at an insane rate. During this time, I made a significant amount of money flipping properties with a relatively low amount of effort. I developed a portfolio of properties and regularly added more properties to it. Then, one day, I looked at my paperwork and realized that I'd done it. I'd become a millionaire. It was somewhat surreal as I sat there and realized I'd get no ticker-tape parade and no congratulations—literally nothing happened.

LOSING IT ALL

I was twenty-eight years old with a portfolio of properties and a net worth of more than a million dollars on paper. However, in hindsight, I realize now that achieving my goal so early was both a blessing and a curse. *How*, you might wonder, *could being a millionaire be a curse?*

The curse was this: Once I hit my milestone, I took my foot off the gas pedal. Without an objective driving me to hustle, I grew complacent, even lazy. I should have asked, "What's next?" then readjusted and set another goal, but I didn't.

I did not know it at the time, but a quote from James Clear, author of *Atomic Habits*, aptly applies to my life at that time: "Goals are for people who care about winning once. Systems are for people who care about winning repeatedly."

I did a good job of setting a direction I wanted to move in and a goal, but I had failed to build a system that became repeatable. You see this often as people set a goal to lose a certain amount of weight and then quickly gain it all back plus some more. The same applies to all aspects of life and especially in investing.

At this point in my story, I'd become a millionaire before thirty and then proceeded to lose it all. "How?" you might ask.

The hard truth is, I lost the money by sitting on my laurels. The subprime bubble burst and the meltdown began. Phoenix was one of three major epicenters in which the subprime bubble burst the hardest—Vegas, Phoenix, and large parts of Florida—where home values fell faster and deeper than anywhere else because they had such an over-supply of new houses. I was too young and naive to see the big picture of what was happening, and instead of acting strategically, I watched everything spin out of control.

It felt like the market was falling by the minute, so I sold my properties as fast as possible to minimize losses. But that meant selling for less than I owed. For example, I owed $300,000 on a property, but I sold it for $275,000. Essentially, I came to the closing table with a $25,000 check and paid the buyer just to get rid of the house. I repeated this process over and over, but the market fell so fast that I ran out of money before I was able to liquidate the portfolio.

I remember sitting on a street curb in Tucson one day at my lowest point. I was subletting an apartment. I dreaded every phone call as bill collectors and lenders lined up and even family and friends, all asking what was happening to the money they had invested with me. I was eighty-five pounds overweight from years of enjoying the good life and eating out in excess. The girl I thought I was going to marry had broken up with me because, to be honest, I was a miserable, depressed person at the time. After the housing market crashed, I'd tried to get back into construction to make some money. I was trying to do *anything* to hang in there, but the world around me was collapsing, and it felt like there was nothing I could do. So I sat on the street curb feeling sick and sleep deprived, and I said a prayer: "I wish I had no money—a net worth of zero."

I didn't have the audacity to pray to be worth a million again, but I wanted to wipe the slate clean and free myself from the debt. To have a net worth of zero instead of being stuck in the hole I had dug for myself would feel like a miracle.

REINVESTING IN A RECESSION

Part of what you'll learn in this book is that the best time to invest in commercial real estate is when there's a recession—when there's blood in the street. At this moment in my story, the blood in the street was mine. I'd gone from being a millionaire to a *negative* worth of hundreds of thousands of dollars. I'd fallen so far into debt and become so overleveraged that I wished and prayed to go back to zero.

My properties were underwater, worth less than what I'd paid for them, and I realized I had to let the portfolio go. A couple of my properties ultimately went into foreclosure, and I tried to short sell them before that played out. However, the market had fallen into such a spiral that nobody knew what was going on. As banks failed, mortgages became lost, and I spent hours on the phone trying to keep my situation from getting worse, all to no avail.

Just as hindsight showed me that becoming a millionaire

was partially a curse, I can look back now and see that the crash in 2008 was somewhat of a blessing. It was an event that happened *for* me, not *to* me. I say this because sometime after my low point on the street curb, I moved back to California. I started working in construction again, making money and recovering. Around this time, a college roommate of mine who worked for a real estate family office reached out. With an abundance of deeply discounted properties from the crash in the market, they were thinking about getting into house flips. Since I had some experience in that area, he wanted to know if I'd be willing to help them.

I agreed to work with them, and by 2009, I started reinvesting myself. Getting back into the market was intimidating after watching everything collapse, but deep down, I knew that this was what I wanted to do for the rest of my life. Although most sane people likely would have given up after the experiences I had been through over a period of only a couple of years, I realized more than anything, I wanted to be back in the game. I couldn't give up on the first major obstacle—I had to pick myself back up and move forward.

Over the following decade, I went on to read hundreds of books on real estate, complete a master's degree in international real estate, get a broker's license, and develop my skillset further. I've done over a thousand flips in twenty-three states and hundreds of millions of dollars of deals using many lessons and trials. In 2014, I founded a private equity real estate investment company that invests primarily in the urban core of secondary cities.

I went from millionaire to negative thousands of dollars and back again. Today, I'm worth several times more than I was before, due in no small part to investments I made after the 2008 recession, which have now compounded. But this book is not meant to chronicle all the deals that went well for me. It is a guide to help you benefit from some of the lessons I learned the hard way and to show you how to avoid them for yourself as you venture into distressed real estate investing.

The key lesson I took away from my experience is this: There will be more recessions in the future. The particulars about which asset classes fall or what markets are affected will differ from recession to recession, but the same principles apply. If you're prepared to act and you have this guide to follow, you can overcome your fears and make a fortune in distressed commercial real estate.

The greatest fortunes can be made by catching "falling knives," the once-in-a-generation opportunities to buy commercial real estate at a deeply discounted price. The phrase is more often used as a warning in the stock markets: "Don't try to catch falling knives," which advises against buying an investment as it rapidly drops in value. The phrase tells investors to instead wait until a price has hit the floor or "bottomed out" before buying in.

However, unlike the stock market, where you have an abundance of choice and can buy as many stocks as you want with the click of a button, commercial real estate involves much more scarcity. An office building or hotel in your target market might go into distress only once a decade or so. You need to be able to reach out and catch those knives when they fall because otherwise, you could miss the once-in-a-lifetime opportunity entirely. Even if a property's price is still actively falling, with a proper plan, you can catch the knife without being cut and benefit from a tremendous rebound in valuation.

YOUR PATH TO FINANCIAL FREEDOM

Now that I've shared a brief part of my story, I want to talk about yours. Why should you invest in commercial real estate? How will this path improve your life?

First and foremost, this book is not a "get rich quick" or "no money down" way to buy real estate. It's a guide based on experiences I have gathered from other investors, mentors, and my own journey—both successes and, certainly, mistakes—to hopefully provide a reliable, proven strategy to successfully invest in distressed commercial real estate.

The main benefit of commercial real estate investing is one that most people can appreciate: financial freedom. There are many ways to financial freedom, including business ownership, stock investing, or even having rich relatives give you a trust fund. But the reality is that real estate investing is one of the few ways that is easy enough to do even part time while you still have a regular day job. In my experience, too many friends and clients feel unsatisfied with their jobs and lives. A lot of people followed the rules and did what they were told they were supposed to do—go to college, get the right degree, work in corporate America or start their own business—and yet their time isn't their own. They work forty, fifty, or sixty hours a week, and it doesn't stop until they retire. Even the most conventionally successful among us often suffer the same constraints.

DOCTOR PAIN

This story might hit home for some of you: I had a client who, by most measures, was a successful person. He was a highly regarded surgeon who owned a practice and made a high six figures—and sometimes even seven figures—in his annual W2 income, but he was so busy that his work got in the way of his quality of life. The worst example was a toothache that started small. The surgeon would go into the office early, perform surgeries back to back all day long, and then with a mountain of paperwork and insurance forms, work until seven or eight at night most weekdays. With his packed schedule, he couldn't get in to see a dentist, as most dentists don't work nights or weekends (*maybe an untapped niche out there for you dentist folks*). Week after week went by, and before too long, months had passed while he ignored the tooth.

Eventually, his dental situation became a significant problem. The pain had grown so severe that he had to take time off work and get the tooth fixed. Instead of a quick fix, it turned into a huge dental procedure. Again, by society's standard measures, this surgeon was quite successful. He had a big house in the right neighborhood and a nice, new car, and he made hundreds of thousands a year. But he was so consumed with a busy schedule that for months, he couldn't take a single afternoon for himself and his own health because he had no freedom from work.

At some point, most of us reach a crossroads where we look around and wonder if the quintessential American dream is worth it if, at the end of the day, we're still trapped on a hamster wheel. Even with a fancier car and large house, how free are you if something happened and you lost two paychecks? How long could you last with your current lifestyle if you lost your job? Would you have to tap into savings or a retirement account to keep from falling behind on the mortgage?

Many people are on a bigger, fancier hamster wheel than

the one we were on when we were younger, but we still have to grind away at the job every day. If the work stops, the money stops. If this describes you and your situation, you might be at that crossroads. You're questioning whether the stress and the hours away from your family are worth it, and you're looking for another option. Along the way, your search has led to real estate investing. Maybe you have a friend or colleague who talks about real estate and takes month-long vacations. You've begun to ask, "How can I do that?"

Like me, your friends and acquaintances might have invested after the 2008 recession, bought real estate at a deep discount, and made millions of dollars. But your opportunity is still ahead of you. Another recession is inevitable, and by learning about investing and preparing to act, you'll be ready when the time comes.

This path can lead you to financial freedom, which doesn't mean you *have* to quit your job—it means you *can*. You'll have the freedom to choose how you spend your time, whether that's working sixty hours a week, three days a week, investing full time, or any other combination of work, leisure, and other pursuits. Would you like to travel more with your partner? Maybe start a charity? For some people, it means having the freedom to coach their kid's sports team. Whatever your why is, you can get off the hamster wheel and live life the way you want.

WHAT YOU'LL LEARN

My goal is for this book to serve as a starting point for your commercial real estate journey. It will give you an overview of the field and, hopefully, spark an interest in you that you decide to pursue further. I'll share general investing principles and philosophy that you can apply in any recession to find and land the best deals. You'll also learn about the following:

- Why a recession is the best time to invest in commercial real estate.
- How commercial real estate investing can create financial freedom.
- Reasons your investing process should start with an exit strategy.
- Strategies for estimating the value of a property.
- Why foreclosures offer some of the best deals and how to find them.
- Creative ways to finance your purchases.
- Red flags in properties and mistakes to avoid.
- How to create an investment team.
- Strategies for finding the most lucrative opportunities.

As you'll see illustrated by both theory and real-life examples, recessions present the greatest opportunity for investing at a discount. To benefit the most from these times, your objective will be to find properties with the widest divide between intrinsic value, aka "what it's worth," and purchase price. In other words, you don't want to buy things for what they are worth; you want to buy them at a discount or "buy low and sell higher." To do this, you'll need to understand the processes and mechanisms that determine market value at any given time. You'll have to differentiate between a bad deal and a great one.

To get to where I am today, I had to go through a lot of ups and downs. It's my hope that by sharing my knowledge, you can save yourself time and stress on your journey to financial freedom. This book won't cover *all* the points and details of commercial real estate investing, but it can give you a guide and a starting point to be ready to act when the next recession strikes.

If you're ready to learn how to catch knives, let's get started.

CHAPTER ONE

THE BEST TIME TO BUY

Buy when there is blood in the streets, even if the blood is your own.

—BARON ROTHSCHILD

Professional investors are like card-counting blackjack players. I mean card counting at a sophisticated level, like the kind highlighted in the book *Busting Vegas* by Ben Mezrich, which describes a group of MIT students who work together to exploit the casinos. Without going into the details of how they did it, the goal of counting cards is to track the cards left in the deck to understand when the deck has more face cards and aces coming up, meaning it is statistically in their betting favor. Professional investors can look at real estate market cycles and discern whether there are more face cards or aces coming up. They know when to bet big, split tens, double down, hit, or stand.

But you don't need to be a professional investor to know that during recessions, the deck is stacked in your favor. The reason is that during these time periods, you can buy assets at a much more significant discount than you can during a booming market. However, even though statistically the deck is stacked in your favor, those card-counting blackjack players know that there isn't a certainty of what is going to happen next. Coincidentally, a recession doesn't guarantee success either. The opportunity lies in undervalued properties, which is why recessions are the best time to buy. In fact, if you make good investments in any recession, it's not unheard of to get a return of over 100 percent.

This book will focus on how you can have a system in place and provide a margin of safety to get the best deals during these market periods and make the largest profits while the deck is stacked most in your favor.

RECESSIONS DON'T REPEAT, BUT THEY DO RHYME

The economy has seen many different recessions over the decades. There have been recessions led by the Great Depression, war, the national bank failures, the savings-and-loan crisis and subsequent Resolution Trust Corporation, a recession following the introduction of real estate investment trusts (REITs) and subsequent over-building, the dot-com bubble burst, and most recently and recognized, subprime bubble bursting. Although these are macro-national-level recessions, sometimes you have more micro- or specific-market recessions, such as Detroit and the auto industry collapse or oil fields going boom and bust. Each recession has unique qualities, but although recessions never repeat exactly, they all tend to rhyme. They have certain similarities that allow you to invest in any recession and earn a profit.

The overarching principle of most recessions is an oversupply in the market of a particular asset class. Most of the time, speculating and overbuilding, and sometimes a shift in demand, is what causes the market to change. When people realize that we've built too many office buildings (houses, apartments, retail spaces, or any other asset type) and that the supply greatly outweighs the demand, the market collapses. Pricing corrects over time until it eventually settles back into a new equilibrium. Nearly every recession follows this same pattern. The time period of the correction, when prices are lower than they will ultimately settle on, is the best time to buy.

BLOOD IN THE STREETS

Baron Rothschild, an eighteenth-century British nobleman and member of the Rothschild banking dynasty (you know, the Illuminati-type people), was the first person credited with saying, "Buy when there's blood in the streets, even if the blood is your own."

He knew the value of buying during recessions—of acting when other people hesitate due to market uncertainty and turmoil. His family made a fortune after the Battle of Waterloo and the panic in the market. If you can overcome your own fears and position yourself to buy during these times, the risks can pay off enormously. The strategy comes back to the enduring principle of buying low and selling high.

One of Rothschild's descendants, Baron Nathan Rothschild, gave equally valuable advice with a twist on this concept: *"Fortunes are made by buying low and selling too soon."*

What did Rothschild mean by "too soon"?

It's difficult, if not impossible, to time the markets perfectly. As the market falls, it's hard to tell where the bottom will be, and when it rises, it's difficult to predict the top. With this in mind, Rothschild took the practical approach of setting a price at which he committed to buying or selling. In other words, once the market hit a certain point, that was his trigger for selling, even if it ended up being "too soon."

In taking this approach, Rothschild avoided a common problem among investors. Often, people become enamored with seeing the market—and their portfolio value—rise. They don't want to let go. I fell into the same trap before the 2008 crash when I saw how much my properties were appreciating. I started holding on to properties even with negative or no cash flow instead of following the plan to sell, and my portfolio grew larger and larger. When the market crashed, the portfolio could not sustain itself without positive cash flow, and I lost everything. If, instead, I'd sold while the market was still rising and had followed my plan, I'd have been sitting on millions of dollars of cash by the time the collapse hit. In short, I'd have gone into the recession in a much better position.

I have taken this concept to heart and come up with a saying: *"You never go broke taking a profit."*

As I have learned, as have many others much smarter and more experienced than me, trying to time the market is the wrong approach. Instead, fortunes are made by buying low and selling "too soon," as Baron Rothschild advised. You want to have a plan for when to exit so you can get out too soon instead of missing your window. Your plan will vary depending on the property you're buying, how you're buying it, and what other needs you have. For example, if you need liquidity in a few months, you might plan to buy a property in extreme distress and quickly sell it to a developer for a profit. Alternatively, a plan with a longer time frame might include buying a property and, over the course of several years, rezoning and rehabbing it and then renting it out.

The most important guideline, which I'll explain in depth in Chapter 3, is to have a plan and start with the end in mind. In other words, have your exit strategy before you buy.

RECESSION INVESTING REQUIRES PATIENCE

You can make a fortune by investing in distressed commercial real estate, but it won't happen overnight. Again, this is not a get-rich-quick scheme; it's a get-rich-over-time strategy. The case study below illustrates a quick return, and although that scenario is a possibility, it's uncommon. To find the best deals, purchase at the greatest discounts, and get the maximum effect from your investing efforts, you need to be prepared to act in times of distress. It's difficult, and sometimes impossible, to predict recessions, which means you also need patience.

For example, nobody could have foreseen that the COVID-19 pandemic would happen, resulting in thirty million people becoming unemployed and the government printing a tremendous amount of money to incentivize economic growth. We can tell when a recession has begun, when economic turmoil is starting to grow, but recessions of this nature aren't predictable. We can't tell when the next recession will happen or how long it will last, only that months or years in the future, another recession will inevitably happen.

CASE STUDY: $4 MILLION TO $8 MILLION IN THIRTY DAYS

In 2009, a subdivision in Lincoln, California, of finished lots went up for sale at a foreclosure auction in the Placer County parking lot. The builder had completed approximately one hundred lots with finished streets and sidewalks, but because of the 2008 housing collapse, the houses themselves had never been built. Now the bank was selling the properties to the highest and best bid with an opening cash bid of $4 million. That averaged out to $40,000 per lot.

The investor group I was working with looked at the deal. We analyzed the property and felt like it was a good price, but with only a few days' notice until the auction, we had to scramble to pull comps and values. Ultimately, the day of the auction arrived, and it was time to decide: do we bid the $4 million or not?

Short answer: We got cold feet and decided not to buy. The bank took the property back as an REO (real estate owned) for the $4 million opening price and listed it on the market. Thirty days later, they sold the lots to KB Homes for $8 million. Had we been better prepared, we could have taken the deal and doubled the investment in only a month.

For us, this was a lesson in how trepidation can cost you and how if you find a good deal, you want to pull the trigger. We found ourselves asking those "woulda, coulda, shoulda"-type questions, such as, "If we coulda been able to do more research on market value, would we have bought?" I think we would have felt comfortable enough with the scenario to make a different decision. We vowed to be better prepared next time, but that next time never materialized, at least in that market.

This deal also illustrated how recessions could create opportunities for significant discounts. The property had

> such a low opening bid price only because the reces-
> sion had interrupted the builder's plans and forced the
> property into foreclosure. Without the crash, the builder
> would have finished constructing the houses and sold
> them off at market value.
>
> I've since done similar deals with returns of 100 percent
> or higher. Although you need to know what to look for
> to find these deals, you can count on them existing in
> nearly every recession.

The unpredictability of recessions is what makes readiness so critical to investing success. You must be prepared to act when the next recession strikes; otherwise, you risk missing the opportunity. Usually, you'll have only a small window in which to act, so every moment counts. You'll want to do the legwork of understanding the market and pricing beforehand so you can quickly judge whether a property is a good deal or not.

CATCH FALLING KNIVES

As I described in the Introduction, recessions present the opportunity to "catch falling knives," the rare chance to buy a property for far lower than its value. This differs from the advice commonly given about the stock market: "*Don't* try to catch falling knives."

To illustrate the difference between the stock market and the real estate market, imagine that you buy a share of

Tesla for $500, but it quickly falls to $300. That's a bad situation because, ideally, you'd want to wait until the price bottoms out at $300 before buying in, at which point you could buy as many shares as you want. However, in commercial real estate (and real estate in general), there's not a nearly unlimited supply of properties available like there are stocks. You might find an office building in San Antonio, or whichever market you're interested in, falling in value or coming into distress only once a decade. You may not have the luxury of waiting until the price bottoms because there is only one property. All you would need is one other interested buyer to purchase it and your opportunity would be over. Like in the case study above, we vowed we would be ready for the next foreclosure sale of finished lots, but that opportunity never happened again—you need to catch the knife while it's falling.

Even if the value of a property is still declining when you buy, as long as you buy at a discount from its fair market value (FMV) or after repair value (ARV), you'll have the opportunity to benefit from the tremendous rebound in valuation when the recession ends. Scarcity plays both to your advantage and your disadvantage in real estate. The advantage is that if you can "grab a falling knife" in a strong market, you can reasonably expect the value to rise again. There's only so much land in a given real estate market, so there will always be a demand for property. The disadvantage of scarcity is that you're competing for limited inventory. If there's only a single property in your chosen market that fits your investing criteria—for example, a distressed hotel—it takes only that one other interested buyer to snatch the opportunity away from you. It might be ten years before another distressed hotel comes on the market. Whereas with stocks, if ten people believe Tesla is underpriced right now and decide to buy, you can come in as the eleventh, hundredth, or thousandth person and still purchase that stock.

With commercial real estate, you can't always wait for a price to bottom out—it's more important to beat the competition and close a good deal while it's available. That's not to say you should rush your decisions but rather to emphasize the importance of being prepared to execute your investment plan when the right opportunity presents itself.

RECOGNIZING OTHER TYPES OF DISTRESS

Throughout this book, I'll focus on recessions as the best opportunities for commercial real estate investing because they result in market-wide distress, but you can leverage small, localized instances of distress as well.

Distress happens during healthy markets whenever something goes wrong for a property owner. Maybe the owner goes through a divorce, accrues medical bills, inherits a property they don't know how to manage, or loses their primary income stream. In any case, something happens that compels them to quickly sell their property—at a discount, if necessary. If you have a plan in place and are ready to act, you can be the person to buy their property at a discount.

Distress can also happen on a larger, but still local, scale if, for example, the factory that employs many residents of a town closes. All of a sudden, nearby restaurants lose their lunch business and also need to close, causing the commercial properties to go into foreclosure. Those properties will then come back onto the market at a deeply discounted price.

These types of isolated deals can occur anywhere and at any time, but again, I'll focus mainly on recessions because it's during these periods when *many* deals will be available all at once. Discounts abound during recessions, making recessions the best time to buy.

BE AN INVESTMENT CONTRARIAN

Along with being patient, success in distressed commercial real estate investing involves being a bit of a contrarian. To get the best bargains, you have to go against the crowd and follow investment strategies that other people are either too afraid of or too unaware to take.

To get ahead, you can leverage two significant emotions

that factor into all of investing: fear and greed. There's the fear of missing out (FOMO) on an opportunity and the fear of losing your money, and there's the greed of holding on to investments too long as I discussed earlier in this chapter. Most people don't control these emotions and instead let them influence their decisions. However, if you can wield them to your advantage, you can make a fortune during recessions.

The best way to control fear and greed is by having a plan and committing to follow it. When you don't have a plan, it's easy to give in to your emotions because you have nothing else guiding your choices. When the fear of failure becomes overwhelming, you buckle. But a plan keeps you on track and sets rules for how you invest. It moves you forward despite fear and also prevents greed from convincing you to hold on to properties for too long.

Many people, myself included years ago, feel scared when they first start in real estate investing because they don't know what to do. I overcame this fear by researching and learning all I could before making my first investment. But the reality is that 80–90 percent of people will never get over their fear—they won't succeed in real estate investing because they'll never even start. Instead, they'll opt for the same investment vehicles as everyone else: stocks, bonds, REITs, and others. There's nothing wrong with these options, but they don't hold the same potential for enormous returns on your investment that you can get from distressed real estate investing. Remember, recessions present the greatest opportunity for deals *because* there's blood in the streets. Most people will be too afraid of the uncertainty to act. By being part of the herd—an average investor—they cannot expect to outperform the markets and get a different outcome. You need to act differently to get exceptional results: be a contrarian.

To be clear, you will always feel *some* fear and uncertainty because investing always involves *some* level of risk. Especially during recessions, nobody knows for sure what the future holds. In the middle of a recession, it might feel like the market will never recover. The goal is not to eliminate fear entirely but to minimize negative emotions and the risk that feeds them by having a plan.

In later chapters, I've laid out a guide to creating your investing plan, which will help you overcome fear, prepare you to take action during the next recession, and set you up to earn the financial freedom you want. The why is your motivation to achieve financial freedom and will be your first defense against fear. It's a goal you can focus on *right now*, before we even get into the more technical details of real estate investing, and your why can give you the courage you need to take the next step toward getting off the hamster wheel.

Stepping off the hamster wheel isn't comfortable—if it were, everyone would do it—but with knowledge, you'll gain the confidence and direction you need to take your first steps. You can read about eating healthy and working out all you want, but unless you actually eat healthily and work out, you won't see the results. It's the same thing for financial freedom. You can read this book and others, but until you take action, you won't see any results.

TIPS AND TAKEAWAYS: THE BEST TIME TO BUY

- Recessions are the best time to invest in commercial real estate because you can get the biggest discounts. During recessions, many people will be afraid to act or will be overleveraged and compelled to sell property under value.
- If you can overcome your own trepidation during recessions, you can "catch knives," the once-in-a-decade opportunities to buy distressed property for far lower than it's worth, and you can make a fortune.
- Discounts caused by isolated instances of distress can happen anywhere and at any time, but you'll find the most opportunities for good deals during recessions.
- Every recession is unique, but they tend to follow a similar pattern: they're almost all caused by an oversupply of a particular asset class followed by a crash in price and, eventually, a correction and new equilibrium.
- Recessions often aren't predictable, so you can't time

them. Instead, you should be ready to act when opportunity strikes. This means being patient and having an investment plan prepared ahead of time.

- Succeeding in commercial real estate investing means being a bit of a contrarian. It's not comfortable going against the crowd, but in doing so, you can earn returns that far outweigh the average.

CHAPTER TWO

CREATE FINANCIAL FREEDOM

Time is more valuable than money. You can get more money, but you cannot get more time.

—JIM ROHN

Investing in distressed commercial real estate offers some of the greatest opportunities for profit. You prepare, wait for a recession, and catch knives when they fall. But now that you know when to act, it's equally important to realize *why* you're acting.

Why should you put in the hard work of learning about distressed real estate? Why push yourself through the risk and uncertainty of buying when there's blood in the street? Why act when most people are too afraid to make a move?

The answer is financial freedom.

THE FREEDOM TO DO WHAT YOU WANT

There's not a person alive who wouldn't prefer to have the money to do what they want, when they want. Yet, so many people—even highly successful professionals like the surgeon from the Introduction—are beholden to their jobs. They don't feel fulfilled by their work or personal lives despite "following the rules" and pursuing the traditional American dream. They went to school, got a good job, married, and bought a house with a white picket fence, but they're still putting forty, fifty, or sixty hours a week into their work. That's not freedom, and as Warren Buffett famously said, "If you don't find a way to make money while you sleep, you will work until you die."

Financial freedom doesn't necessarily mean that you dislike your job and want to quit. It simply means that you have the *freedom* to choose how much time you want to put into your job, whether that's fifty hours a week, fifteen, or none at all. The point is that you get to decide how you spend your time. For one person, financial freedom might mean taking more vacations. For someone else, maybe it's having a two-day workweek. For yet another, it's finding the time to work out every day. Freedom means something different to everyone, and before you start your real estate journey, I recommend figuring out what it means to you.

WHAT DOES FINANCIAL FREEDOM LOOK LIKE TO YOU?

Like I've said, being a contrarian isn't easy, so you'll want a clear motivation and goal to get you through moments of doubt. To gain a solid grasp on your motivation for investing in commercial real estate, ask yourself the following questions:

- What would I do if I had financial freedom?
- Would I work less at my current job?
- Would I work the same amount but free up time by hiring an assistant or housekeeper?
- Would I switch careers?
- Would I retire?
- Would I pay off all my debt?
- Do I want to travel more?
- Would I give back to church or charity?
- Are there big purchases I'd like to be able to afford?

To me, the definition of being rich or wealthy is being able to answer these questions and make those answers a reality. A retired schoolteacher with a steady retirement income and no debt has the freedom to do what they want and is wealthier, in this way, than an executive living in a large house who has to work sixty hours a week to afford their lifestyle. That's because the schoolteacher living off their retirement investments has something the executive doesn't: passive income that's greater than their expenses.

True wealth and freedom come from not depending on your job or the state of the economy to maintain your daily lifestyle.

PASSIVE INCOME: MAKING MONEY IN YOUR SLEEP

I've been fortunate that through my own errors, I've had opportunities for introspection—moments after falling flat on my face where I stopped and asked, "What does freedom mean to me?"

I knew that passive income would play a large role in my personal definition of freedom, and it probably does for you, too. Passive income is the tool that gives you access to all kinds of other freedoms because it isn't limited by your waking hours—it's making money in your sleep.

The best way to think about passive income relative to your normal job is horizontal income versus vertical income. Horizontal income is money you make while you're horizontal, aka sleeping. For example, it's the rent you collect on the buildings you own. It does not require your direct input to generate wealth.

Vertical income requires your active participation. You're standing or sitting at a computer, or wherever else your job requires you to be, whether you're a doctor, lawyer, or other professional. Vertical income can bring in a lot of money, but it is trading your time for money. If you aren't working, you aren't earning.

Vertical income keeps you on the hamster wheel, but the horizontal income generated by investing in distressed commercial real estate can bring you true financial freedom. The passive income it generates will give you more flexibility in how you spend your days, and most importantly, it will remove the gun from your head that keeps you working sixty hours a week to pay the bills.

WHY COMMERCIAL REAL ESTATE INVESTING?

Commercial real estate is by no means the only way to earn passive income, but if you understand how the business works, it's one of the most significant ways to generate financial freedom.

How does it measure up to other investment options?

Let's look at the pros and cons of three common ways to invest—stocks, residential real estate, and commercial real estate—to compare the differences.

Stocks

Pro: A lower barrier to entry

Anyone with a smartphone or laptop can start investing in the stock market for mere dollars, making it the easiest option for most investors. The popular investment app Robinhood has even opened up options trading to the masses, and many millennials have jumped into the stock market.

Con: High volatility

Of these three investment classes, stocks have the most volatility. Something as simple as Elon Musk going on a Twitter rampage in the middle of the night can send Tesla's stock price tumbling. The media and public opinion both influence a stock's valuation, and as a stock investor, there's nothing you can do to anticipate or prevent such fluctuations.

Residential Real Estate

Pro: A lower barrier to entry

Residential real estate investing requires less money compared to commercial real estate. You can get started with only a little, or even none, of your own money. That's why I started in residential real estate investing in my twenties: I needed only about $10,000 to buy my first property.

Con: High rental turnover and more competition

If you own a residential rental property, it's not unusual to have tenant turnover every twelve months. This requires more legwork to find and screen new tenants, as well as weeks or months between leases where the property possibly sits empty. Naturally, more time spent managing tenants means less freedom in how you spend your time overall. The low cost of entry also drives significant competition and ultimately drives down the profit margins as more people chase fewer "deals."

Commercial Real Estate

Pro: One of the top-performing asset classes

Commercial real estate regularly outperforms other investment options such as stocks and residential real estate. In fact, return values have more than doubled since 2009.

Pro: Relatively low risk

The risk and volatility associated with commercial real estate tend to be lower compared to other options, which is especially important if you plan to invest a significant portion of your life savings. You want to be as confident as possible that you won't lose money. Part of this lower risk is due to private commercial real estate not trading on public markets, making it somewhat disconnected from the usual fluctuations of publicly traded equities.

Pro: More stable income stream

With residential rental properties, your tenants likely sign an annual lease, which means every year, you either need to re-sign with them or find new tenants. With commercial properties, there tends to be less turnover. It's not unusual for renters to sign a three-, seven-, ten-, or even twenty-year lease, giving you a more stable, predictable passive income stream.

Con: A higher barrier to entry

The downside to commercial real estate investing is that it requires a much higher amount of capital compared to either stocks or residential real estate. Deals typically transact for millions, or even hundreds of millions, or billions, of dollars. Most people don't have the capital for that level of investing. That said, there are ways to gain access to the necessary capital, even if you don't have it in the bank: invest into a fund, syndication, or group to buy a property together.

Con: Less liquidity

With stocks, you can buy and sell almost anytime you want, whereas commercial real estate sales take more time to transact. Valuations also tend to be much more glacial in terms of pricing movement because properties change hands far less often than stocks or residential homes.

KNOW YOUR INVESTMENT

As you can see, commercial real estate offers several advantages that stocks and residential real estate lack, but to succeed, you need to know what you're doing. Buying a multimillion-dollar commercial property gives you less room for error than, say, buying a few thousand dollars' worth of Tesla stocks. You'll want to know how to valuate properties, how you can convert or reuse buildings to raise their value, how to identify growing markets, where to find the best deals, and more—all of which we'll explore in subsequent chapters.

CHANGE CREATES OPPORTUNITY

There's never been a better time in history for the average person to achieve financial freedom, and it's largely due to technology changing the world. We're seeing unprecedented shifts in the way we do things, including how we invest our money.

In the past, commercial real estate deals primarily stayed restricted to tight circles of wealthy investors—institutional investors, hedge funds, and then trickling down to the "country club crowd," you might say. But why should the already-rich be the only ones allowed to reap the rewards of commercial real estate?

They shouldn't, and with the opportunities created by

changing laws and technology, they aren't. For instance, in 2012, President Obama signed the Jumpstart Our Business Startups Act, or JOBS Act, to help open up investments to more people via investment vehicles known as crowdfunding. Today, you no longer need to be a member of the ultra-elite mastermind groups or the country club to access the same deals that have historically made the rich richer. That said, there is nothing wrong with being in masterminds and country clubs, as I have found being around like-minded people has helped expand my own knowledge. But you don't *need* to be part of that crowd to start investing. Today, anyone with the knowledge, motivation, and starting money can get involved through crowdfunding and group investments. Thanks to the internet and social media, investors can solicit other investors from around the world, form groups, and buy larger properties than any single member of the group could afford on their own. Group investors may not have the level of control they'd have as a solo investor, but by buying into a fund, they can still get a piece of the pie formerly reserved for the investing elite.

Another way technology has disrupted commercial real estate is by making it easier than ever to find property deals. For example, in the past, if you wanted to find foreclosures in your market, you'd have to skim the local newspaper or check with the county recorder's office for public notices. Once you found a foreclosure, you might have to go dig through the records and pull out microfiche of the property's title at the county recorder's office. Everything happened manually, and to be a player in a market, you needed someone on the ground checking local notices for new deals. Obviously, this made it difficult for small, non-institutional investors to get involved anywhere outside their own backyard. Then the internet changed everything.

Today, you can find almost every public notice and foreclosure listing online as more and more counties digitize their records. So as long as you have a connection to the internet, you could be on a beach in the Caribbean browsing available foreclosures in downtown Cincinnati that look appealing to you (as it happens, I am editing this book on a beach in the Caribbean). You don't need an associate headquartered in each market you're operating in because you can now operate everywhere. As technology continues to develop, access to real estate for the average investor should only get better, too.

The change brought about by technology creates opportunities in investing, but it also causes fear. The human brain doesn't react well to unknown stresses and rapid change—in the distant past, a changing environment meant an insecure food supply, and the unknown meant a saber tooth tiger was jumping out and eating you. Our brains are hardwired to be anxious, alert, and on the lookout for danger, and the rapid iteration of technology triggers those stress signals.

Change causes fear just like recessions, but as I discussed earlier, if you're able to overcome your fear, you can seize the opportunities that other people miss. Catch falling knives, and you'll enjoy a tremendous rebound in value once other people adapt to the change and the prices correct.

Commercial real estate isn't your only path to financial freedom, but it's one of the best and most efficient ways I have found to grow your wealth and generate a passive income, especially during periods of economic uncertainty and change.

TIPS AND TAKEAWAYS: CREATE FINANCIAL FREEDOM

- Everyone wants the financial freedom to do what they want, whether that's working less, traveling more, buying a bigger house, or anything else. Freedom means something different to everybody—figure out what it means to you.
- One of the best ways to gain financial freedom is through commercial real estate investing. This investment path can earn you passive income, meaning you'll make money in your sleep. Passive income is the only way to unchain your time from your paycheck.
- Commercial real estate has a few advantages over other investment options, such as stocks and residential real

estate: higher returns, lower risk, and a more stable income stream.

- The downsides to commercial real estate investing—a high barrier to entry and low liquidity—can be mitigated somewhat by investing through a group fund. By investing in funds, you can start with less capital and spread your money across more properties.
- Changing investment technology has created more opportunities for the average investor than ever before, but like recessions, the uncertainty of new technology also causes fear. Overcome your fear, and you can take advantage of deals that other people are too afraid to pursue.

CHAPTER THREE

START WITH THE END

Investment success doesn't come from "buying good things" but rather from "buying things well."

—HOWARD MARKS

As you've learned so far, commercial real estate investing can earn you massive returns, but in the pursuit, you can also make massive mistakes. The more money you put in, the more money you stand to lose, and while commercial real estate offers lower volatility and risk than most other investment paths, it's not a magic silver bullet.

To maximize your chance of success, you'll want to start with the end: your exit strategy for every property you buy. In real estate, common wisdom says that you make your money when you buy, not when you sell. It's difficult, if not impossible, to turn a bad deal into a good one if you bought it improperly. In other words, if you buy at the wrong price based on the future valuation and cost to get the property there, no amount of effort will make up the difference.

For example, imagine paying $5 million for a building that should be worth $10 million. At face value, it sounds like a good deal. However, after you buy the building, you learn that it needs $10 million of renovations to be habitable. Now, you've put $15 million into a property that's only worth $10 million, and there might not be any way to make up the $5 million loss.

If a piece of property won't sell for more than you paid (and spent fixing it up), you've lost as soon as you've purchased it. After that point, trying to make up the value is a losing game. That's why you want to figure out your end-game strategy and the exit value before buying a piece of property.

Success requires you to consider a property's future valuation and the money required to fix it *before you buy it* so you can avoid unprofitable deals from the start.

DEFINE YOUR INVESTMENT CRITERIA

To "start with the end," you want to first think about your goals and the criteria that will direct your investments.

What is your destination? Where do you want to go? You now know what financial freedom looks like to you, but what is it going to take to get there?

There are three criteria you'll want to consider—financial goals, asset class, and location—that will narrow your focus and determine which deals you consider. Time is your most precious asset, which is why it's so important to figure out your goals now. The investment world is huge, and if you don't whittle down your approach, it can be overwhelming. Setting goals will reduce the number of deals you're considering to a manageable amount and save you time in the long run.

HOW MUCH WILL YOUR DREAM LIFE COST?

Remember when we talked about defining your why in an earlier section? *Why* are you interested in commercial real estate investing? This is an exercise that few people ever complete, but it's worth doing, and the next steps can be life altering.

Break down and quantify what your why, or so-called dream life, costs (*download a dream-life cost template at www. catchknives.com/resources*). If you have already defined your why, this exercise will be easier. If not, then you can still do it, but you'll want to write out on the template or a sheet of paper all the things in your life and then figure out whether those costs are yearly or monthly.

The first step is to write out all the things you want. For example, maybe you want to live in Europe for one month a year. How much does that cost? The answer depends on how many people are coming with you and how lavish or simple you may want to live. A good book for more travel-related cost hacks is *Vagabonding* by Rolf Potts. Or maybe your dream life has a personal chef, a private plane, or the ability to give away $1 million on one of those big paper checks all at once.

By putting numbers into your dream life, you will be able to see your realistic end goal. I know of one person who told their coach they needed to make $2 million per year to have their dream life. When the coach asked them why they needed $2 million, they thought about it and boiled it down to the fact that it sounded like a lot of money. They then decided to reexamine the numbers involved. Once they did this exercise, they were able to see that many of the items on their list were more "nice to have" rather than "need to have." Did they need to own a villa in Italy? Or was it better to rent a villa for three months a year? Ultimately, they figured out that they needed only $650,000 per year to afford their dream life. That might be a lot of money for some, but it was well within reach of this already-high-income earner.

Now, why is this exercise important for catching knives and investing in distressed commercial real estate? It helps you define personally where you need to be and then helps you repeat this process with the type of real estate deals you may want to invest into.

Additionally, I have found that people and their behavior toward money are not as cut and dry as saying, "Here is the math problem; now make this decision," or "Whichever deal pays out more money equals 'I will pick that one.'" For instance, here is something that many can relate to. There is a lot of debate around owning or renting your personal residence. When I was in grad school studying international real estate, I built models evaluating if it made more financial sense to own or rent your home. In many expensive markets, it showed that it was more financially beneficial to rent versus own, and that was heavily skewed toward the lens of only looking at the simple fact of financial sense.

However, I know many people whose knee-jerk reaction is "That sounds wrong." They could never conceive of not owning their own home. As I am assuming we are all human and the robots and AI haven't taken over yet, the human element or emotional factor has to be there when considering your financial goals. What does that mean? Behavioral economics is the study of humans and how we make decisions, and it shows that we are oftentimes predictably irrational. If you want to dive deeper into this subject, I put together a book list at **www.catchknives. com/booklist.**

Here's a synopsis of that subject: People all have different and distinct environments in which they grew up and were raised. The way that we think about money and finances is significantly shaped by those experiences and, oftentimes, requires its own self-discovery process to change our outcomes. That is why I have put together this book—because having a plan, even loosely followed, will better help people build a path to their own financial freedom.

The debate on owning versus renting depends on your own circumstances, and some advisors and gurus will tell you that the secret to wealth is having no debt, with having your house paid off being the key to freedom. However, that is very basic financial advice, and it's important to understand that most people follow it because it makes them feel more secure.

It's important to determine how much your dream life will cost because all of these things will help you build your investment criteria before you start investing and help you with your investing journey.

FINANCIAL GOALS

Next, consider the financial goals you want to meet through commercial real estate investing.

Let's say your financially free dream lifestyle requires a

horizontal (passive) income of $10,000 per month, so your goal is to bring in a certain amount of passive income every month. That's the criterion you'll use to determine what kinds of deals you're looking to make. Every time you look at a property, you'll ask, "Does this bring me closer to $10,000 per month?"

It can be useful to break your goal down further: Do you want to own ten properties bringing in $1,000 per month? Or would you rather own one property that brings in $10,000? If you prefer ten $1,000 properties, you'll be looking at entirely different deals than if you were to go the $10,000 single-property route.

To be clear, your goal doesn't have to center on passive income. For example, your goal might be to accrue a lump sum of $1 million, so you wouldn't be as concerned about receiving a consistent check every month. Instead, you'd look for properties that you could turn around and sell for a huge profit. Do you want to sell ten properties that earn you $100,000 in profit each, or a single deal that pays out $1 million?

Deal Size

While on the topic of what deal size you might want to do, I want to discuss the competition. I have found that there is a certain level of competition worth avoiding. First, keep in mind that most major markets have tiers of competition: the big dogs, which are the "institutional buyers" (sovereign wealth funds, private equity, pension funds, and more), and on the other end of the spectrum, there are the smaller "mom and pop" investors.

The institutional investors are smart. They have sophisticated models, the cheapest cost of capital, and the best of the best talent. It is difficult to beat them at their game, especially for a new investor. However, there is some good news: they avoid small deals. To them, a small deal is anything under $25 million. The reason they avoid small deals is that it requires the same amount of work to do a $1 million deal as it does to do a $100 million deal. Simply put, they don't waste their time with smaller deals. If they make a 30 percent return on a $1 million deal, that is $300,000 profit. But if they make a 30 percent return on a $100 million deal, that is $30 million profit for essentially the same amount of work. If you can do bigger deals, the rewards are significantly greater.

As I mentioned, on the other end of the spectrum, you have what are called mom-and-pop investors, as they typically make investments around what they can personally qualify for or what falls into their lap from local knowledge. They don't typically use investment models or have great access to capital. As a result, they tend to do deals under $1 million to $2 million, depending on the individual market.

Those quick with math have already figured out that there seems to be a niche of opportunity for an investor or group to play where others aren't. That means there is a sweet spot—the best opportunities without institutional competition—below $25 million. In my experience, if you focus on deals between $2 million and $25 million, you'll also avoid competition from the small mom-and-pop or country club investors. By using a plan and system like institutional investors, you'll have greater opportunities to set yourself up for success without competition.

Risk

Going back to your financial goals and how to craft your investment criteria, you'll also want to consider your personal risk tolerance. If your primary driver is "don't lose money," you probably want to stay away from speculative development deals, which have a higher risk profile. On the other hand, if you're open to higher risk in exchange for a chance to achieve above-market returns, you might consider a broader range of options than someone investing conservatively. Your financial goal and risk tolerance will both determine the types of deals you consider.

Last, also consider all the appropriate fees. I see many new investors miss out on things such as carrying cost or underestimating expenses such as transaction cost. One of the main factors with real estate that provides the opportunity for savvy investors is that it is inefficient in trading. That means it costs a lot of money to trade real estate. You will have brokers, title, escrow, recorders, taxes, and more. All in all, expect to pay 5–10 percent of the property's value every time it is traded (bought or sold). In comparison, trading $10 million in stocks might cost only a few dollars in trading fees, whereas a $10 million commercial building might have $1 million in fees.

ASSET CLASS

Another way to narrow your focus is by choosing one or more asset classes to make up the majority of your investments.

For example, some investors find hotels fascinating and choose to invest only in that asset class. Someone else might avoid hotels because they hate the fact that their "renters" are so short term and would be renting rooms in their property every night. That investor might instead focus on distribution centers with long-term leases, mobile homes, apartments, or office buildings. It's important to choose an asset class that aligns with your financial goals because unlike residential real estate, where houses of a similar size on the same street will have similar prices, commercial real estate is a completely different animal. You can't simply pull up Redfin or Zillow and get a ballpark-accurate valuation estimate.

With commercial real estate, you could see one building worth $65 million and another, a similarly sized building next door worth only $5 million. A 12,000-square-foot restaurant will have a different value than a 12,000-square-foot apartment building, for example. The difference is largely due to the capitalization rate (cap rate), which is a measurement of the rate of return expected to be generated on the property. This is calculated by dividing the net operating income by the property asset value. Cap rates and valuations vary widely by asset class, so you'll want to choose an asset class or two based on your financial goals.

As you define your investment strategy, ask yourself, "What types of properties do I like? What kind of returns do I want? What do I want my risk profile to be?"

Limiting your portfolio to select asset classes will allow you to specialize your knowledge in that particular area and spend your time only looking at deals that get you closer to your financial goals. That said, being a true opportunistic generalist is an option, too. You can be agnostic toward asset type and focus solely on finding the best deal possible. However, I don't recommend this approach for new investors because it's difficult to gain knowledge across multiple asset classes that you need to avoid getting burned. You end up being an inch deep and a mile wide. It is better to be immensely knowledgeable in one asset type before branching out to others.

Instead, look into a few asset classes and decide which interests you most. Going down the rabbit hole of commercial real estate deals can take months or more, so you only want to pursue deals that have the greatest likelihood of satisfying your criteria. Remember, time is your most valuable resource. Don't waste it on the wrong deals. Make it your goal to say no to potential deals as fast and efficiently as possible, and you'll see a much better return on your investment of time.

Here are a few quick pros and cons of popular asset types. Keep in mind that this is a snapshot of these assets going into 2021. These are macro-level assessments, as many markets across the country do not experience these pros and cons. Additionally, this does not cover *all* the possibilities of available commercial real estate deals.

Multifamily (MF) Apartments, Five-or-More Units, Garden Style, Urban, Infill

Pros: High leverage rates, long-term low-interest rate possibilities (agency loans, Fannie, Freddie, HUD, and more), high demand from renters, and good demand and low cap rates when you want to sell (sell side), with scale property managers to ease a significant burden of operations.

Cons: Low cap rates equal low returns, high competition on the buy side (meaning you have to pay a lot for the property), short leases of twelve months or less, and hard to self-manage unless you want to receive leaky-toilet calls in the middle of the night.

Office

Pros: Long-term leases, higher cap rates, fewer property management calls versus multifamily, and less competition.

Cons: Work-from-home trend, commercial contractors are more expensive and less available than residential (meaning everything costs more, especially in a value-add scenario; the cost of an elevator can be hundreds of thousands).

Single-Tenant Net Lease (STNL), CVS, Walgreens, Dollar General, and Others

Pros: Low risk as these are treated more like a coupon return and have long-term leases and corporate guarantees. Twenty- to thirty-year leases are typical with built-in increases and require zero landlord responsibility.

Cons: The corporation could fail (e.g., Pier 1, Kmart, and more). When you pay a premium for the lease and then they fail, it reverts back to the intrinsic value of the building. You need to consider how much it costs to build that type of building. If the tenant leaves, what are real market rents?

For instance, an ideal auto parts store may not be desirable to several other users.

Shopping Center, Strip Centers (Retail), Grocery Stores, Gyms, Restaurants

Pros: Very high cap rates equal a good return on investment (ROI), low competition, and can require little landlord involvement.

Cons: Amazon and the proliferation of retail as a whole (you must ask whether the tenants are e-commerce-proof).

Hospitality, Hotels, Motels, Short-Term Rentals

Pros: Great yield (meaning high-income-producing properties), can be very hands-off, multiple streams of income (food and beverage, merchandise), high-status investment, and in my opinion, the commercial property you can use with your family the easiest.

Cons: Subject to tourism whims, travel dips during recessions, you are renting the rooms every single night, hotel operations are expensive and the cost to acquire books are expensive, and it's a business as well as real estate.

Of course, there are more assets to commercial real estate, and this book is not meant to be a fully inclusive breakdown of all of them. I do discuss them in more detail on the website (**catchknives.com**) and on social media platforms.

LOCATION

Last, you'll want to consider locations for your investment properties. Do you want to invest in your hometown? The state you live in? Across the country? How important is it that you're able to regularly visit the property?

People tend to naturally want to invest in their own back-yard. They're familiar with the area and have some amount of market research innately built in: they know the top employers in the area, they know which is the good side of the street and which is the bad side, they know if the area is growing, and more.

Investing in your immediate area isn't necessarily the wrong choice, but it probably isn't the best market available either. For example, when I first started investing, buying a property in California simply wasn't an option because prices were too high. I would have struggled to find a good deal I could afford, whereas in a midsize, growing city like Phoenix, I found plenty of opportunities to buy. If you live in a major metropolitan area like New York City, Los Angeles, Chicago, or Seattle, you might want to consider investing outside of your immediate area.

Real estate in large cities is highly competitive, and you have many of those institutional players and several small and medium players to contend with. Most secondary or tertiary markets won't have the same institutional competition, but those local markets have what I call the mafia rule. Every smaller city tends to have four to five families, like the mafia bosses of yesteryear, that represent an 80–90 percent control of the market and all major deals. Although these families are not the same ruthless mafia types from the movies, it is good to be cautious in your deals, as you don't want to be the out-of-towner who is stuck buying a terrible property that everyone else knows is a dud. But there are many advantages to investing where these families are not; they are often complacent and their local knowledge is a crutch that holds them back.

Also, consider that sometimes your financial goals, asset class, and location won't align. For example, if you've decided you want to invest in office buildings that bring in $3,000 per month in Boise, Idaho, you might find that there aren't any deals in that market that fit your criteria. In this case, you'd have to either adjust your criteria by expanding to a new asset class or market or wait until a deal becomes available. You need to think about whether a market will have enough of your target asset class to buy, and similarly, whether you'll be able to sell the property. You might want to focus on luxury hotels in the market of Shreveport, Louisiana, but if you aren't able to turn around and sell that hotel to anyone in Shreveport after you fix it up, you could lose money. It's the same as building a thirty-story building in Wichita Falls, Kansas. Not only will that project likely be difficult to get financed, but who will buy it?

If it takes you two years to find a buyer, the holding costs are going to cut into your profit margin. A property sitting empty still has costs associated with taxes, utilities, and upkeep. Unless you factor in these additional costs at the beginning, you could be setting yourself up for failure.

Starting with the end means thinking about your exit plan and making sure you'll be able to find a buyer for the right price when you're ready to sell. The asset needs to match the market to be a successful investment, and ideally, you want your property to be as easy to sell as possible.

SET YOURSELF UP FOR SUCCESS

Once you know your goal, market, and the type of deals you're considering—for example, properties that will produce a passive income of $5,000 per month—you can start analyzing potential deals. When you look at a property, the first question you want to ask is, "What will this property be worth when I sell it?"

You want to reverse engineer the deal to figure out the property's future valuation—a process I'll describe in detail in the next chapter.

BUYING AT A DISCOUNT

I discussed it in the first two chapters, but this principle is worth repeating in the context of future valuation: The best way to set yourself up for success is to buy properties for less than they're worth. This is the most dependable way to make money, and it doesn't require significant levels of genius or even superior efforts by the owner. It just requires the market to return to normal.

When you buy at a discount, you have more room for error as you move the property from its current point (the moment you purchase it) to your exit point (the moment you sell it). In the time between those two points, you'll likely need to spend money fixing, renovating, or repurposing the space, and you only have so much you can spend before you eliminate your profits.

Think of investing like walking a tightrope across the Grand Canyon, except when you buy at a significant discount, your rope is only five feet off the ground and you have safety nets. If you fall, you might get scratched up, but you probably won't die. That buffer means you might be able to afford a costly surprise that comes up, such as asbestos in the walls or out-of-code wiring, and still make a profit when you sell.

On the other hand, if you buy a property at value, each extra cost puts you in the red. Even worse, if you buy a property for more than it's worth, you have to beat the market when you sell. Now you're walking across the tightrope fifty feet off the ground with no safety nets, and if you fall, you might die.

UNDERSTANDING MARKET TRAJECTORIES

Buying at a discount becomes especially important if you buy in a declining market—for example, during a recession. Let's say that you're interested in a property that's worth $10 million today, but in a year from now, it will be worth $9 million. To judge whether you can make this deal work, you need to know what you can buy the property for and what it will be worth when you decide to sell it. If you can buy it for $5 million today, you have a lot of room for profit regardless of whether it goes down to $9 million or back up to $10 million. However, if you are buying it for $9 million, you have a smaller window for making a profit. You *need* the property to go back up to $10 million to make a profit. If it instead continues to decline and falls to $8 million, now you may be in a position to lose money. This is a risk you face unless your plan is to hold until it rebounds in pricing, which is not always the case. Some markets can take longer to recover than you can hold on to the property.

Another example might be a property you can buy for $2

million, but the current market says it's only worth $1.5 million. If you're only looking at those two variables, it sounds like a bad deal. However, if you're able to analyze the market's trajectory and predict that the property will be worth $5 million three years from today, it could be a great deal—assuming it won't cost you $3 million to get the value up to $5 million. If your exit strategy involves selling the property three years from now, it doesn't matter what the market value is today or even six months from now. As long as the numbers align with your long-term vision and your exit strategy, the short-term value is irrelevant. You'll still make a profit when you go to sell. The value could drop to $500,000, and it's fine because your investment thesis shows that the market will correct itself and raise the value to $5 million. This bigger-picture view takes into account current valuation, future valuation, cost to improve the property, and market trajectory to give you a more accurate estimate of a deal's worth.

A property's valuation comes down to much more than the cost of the sticks and bricks required to build it. Consider the distressed market of Detroit, where you might buy a building for $50 per square foot. That same building might cost $200 per square foot to build new, but because of the huge supply of vacant buildings and the lack of buyers, the price is lower than the cost of the materials. That market trajectory, plus supply and demand factors, influence property valuations much more than the cost to build.

To avoid losing money on your investments, it's important to understand the market dynamics in your chosen area. How does the supply of properties compare to the demand? A supply that outweighs demand drives down prices. Look around at your target market. Are there twenty-five properties similar to the deal you're considering sitting vacant? If so, why would someone buy this property from you instead of the others? Why would a bank finance your purchase?

In this scenario, you would probably struggle to finance and sell the property. I'm not saying avoid declining markets—as I covered in the previous chapters, distressing conditions hold the most opportunity. Naturally, most recessions will have declining property values, and these conditions are at the core of catching falling knives. The degree and rate of decline vary by market: some markets will have steep declines, and others will have little to no decline. In the most recent subprime housing recessions, areas like San Antonio, Texas, and Buffalo, New York, saw very little decline in property prices, whereas almost all of California, Arizona, and Florida experienced value declines of up to 80 percent, largely driven by a huge run-up in supply and then elimination of demand.

DO YOUR DUE DILIGENCE

Again, I'm not trying to scare you away from declining markets; I'm stressing the importance of due diligence. If you do your research and understand loosely how a deal will likely play out from the time you purchase the property to the moment you sell it, you can make a fortune. But if you don't do your due diligence, you set yourself up for failure.

Success requires considering the following variables:

- The trajectory of the market
- The property's current value
- How you'll finance your purchase
- Transactional cost (typically 10 percent)
- The property's future value
- How much income, if any, the property will generate while you hold it
- The duration you plan to hold the property
- How much you'll need to spend to fix, renovate, or repurpose the property
- How quickly you'll be able to sell the property

You can get a free Due Diligence Checklist at **www.catch knives.com/resources**. With time, you'll develop a more intuitive sense of judging properties and potential deals, but when you're just getting started, it's critical to break these variables down. Take as much of the guesswork out of the equation as you can and do your due diligence, aka homework. If you know an experienced investor, run potential deals by them, too. Many people will be happy to throw down the rope and help you establish your investment portfolio.

CASE STUDY: BUYING A PROPERTY FOR MORE THAN IT IS WORTH

In 2012, Blackstone, the biggest institutional player of them all, came into our market and started buying everything. With a billion-dollar-plus fund specifically targeting the Sacramento market where I was in 2012, it bought everything listed on the market and everything at foreclosure auctions. I stood there watching this team of investors pay any price for properties. In fact, several times, Blackstone even paid more for a property than it was worth. I couldn't understand what was going on. Why would one of the smartest and best real estate investment firms in the world buy something for more than the market value? It went counter to everything I knew.

I was unable to buy any properties because even though we had millions to invest, it didn't matter when Blackstone had billions to invest. With this extra time, I went on a mission to discover why anyone would pay more for a property than it is worth. It took me months to figure out what the company was doing. Blackstone was playing a different game. While I was concerned with what the price was today, it was making investments at a discount of previous market values. Blackstone didn't care what the value was today. Its investors felt like the market would "shoulder" off those previous values and rebound beyond them.

Here's how that works: If a property was worth $500,000 at the 2006 peak, Blackstone was willing to be "all in" on that investment at 70–75 percent of that previous value. Even if that current market value was $250,000, it might pay $300,000 for that property, fix it up for $50,000, and be all in at $350,000, or 70 percent of the previous high. I had a hard time competing because if the property was worth $250,000 fixed up, how could I pay $300,000 before fixing it?

But Blackstone understood the intrinsic value of those properties. It made its investments based on the fact that it could wait until the markets rebounded and that property was worth $550,000 or more before selling it. But for us, who wanted to trade those assets in the next three to six months, it made no sense. However, taking this longer-term hold strategy, Blackstone was able to do that to some 50,000 properties in a few years and earn several billion in profit.

TIPS AND TAKEAWAYS: START WITH THE END

- Commercial real estate investing covers a lot of ground, so you'll want to narrow your focus and specialize in a particular asset class and market.
- The faster you can define what you're looking for—financial goals, asset classes, and location—the more precisely you can consider properties and the less time you'll waste on deals that are irrelevant to you.
- You make your money when you buy, not when you sell. In other words, if you make a deal where the numbers don't line up in your favor, you've already lost the game.
- Fortunes are made by buying low and selling too soon, and in order to buy low, you need three data points: how much it will cost to buy the property now (your starting point), how much money it will take to fix any problems (the distance you need to cover), and how much you can sell the property for in the future (your exit point).
- You can judge the value of a potential deal by starting with your exit strategy. Figure out how much the prop-

erty will be worth when you sell it and whether you can make a profit.

- You can make a fortune by buying in declining markets, but you must do your due diligence to avoid a scenario where you lose money. Make sure the market trajectory will shift and the property's value will rise again by the time you sell.

CHAPTER FOUR

WHAT'S A PROPERTY WORTH?

All that matters in the end is the bottom line.

—SAM ZELL

You walk down the main street of your city and see a row of commercial buildings that all look alike. At first glance, you might assume they're worth the same amount, but their valuations differ immensely. One is worth $1 million, another $5 million, and the third $10 million. As a new investor, if you didn't know their values, how could you possibly know if purchasing one of the buildings was a good deal?

You couldn't. Good deals require knowing what a property is worth, which is why our next step is to take a closer look at how you can determine value.

I often use the Back of the Envelope (BOE) model, which you can find in the resources guide online (**www.catchknives. com/resources**). But before you get one of those guides, let me go into details of the variables you are looking for and ultimately trying to determine. Your ability to predict values will save you a ton of time as you look for your deal.

MEASURING A PROPERTY'S VALUE

A property's current value drives much of the investment process, starting with how much you pay for it. The appraisal calculation takes into account multiple variables:

- The property's physical condition: How old is the building? Is it damaged? Out of code? Worn or outdated?
- The building's replacement value: What is the square footage? What materials were used in the building? How much would it cost to construct an equivalent structure?
- The property's location: What neighborhood is it in? What's next to it?
- The land: How much is the land itself worth? What are the dimensions of the lot?
- The property's income potential: How much income has it generated in the past? How much is it expected to bring in next year?
- The building's use: What is the building's current use (hotel, apartments, retail, or other)? Could it be repurposed in a way that increases the value?

With each of these data points, you get a more accurate, real-world estimate of a property's value, which allows you to predict the profit you'd earn from making the deal.

OLD VERSUS NEW CONSTRUCTION

A good starting point for your valuation is to figure out how much it would cost to construct the same property today. Let's imagine you're considering buying a ninety-year-old, 100,000 square foot office building, and you consult a contractor and learn that a new 100,000 square foot building would cost $20 million to build. That's for new construction, with new finishes, new tile floors, new windows, new HVAC—new everything. If you then factor in the cost of the land, permits, and project timing, you can determine the replacement value. You know, at least, that you have a number you are working to be under.

Let's assume that a new construction model costs $20 million, or $200 per square foot for the building. Assume land and permits and construction interest cost another $10 million, so all in, a new 100,000 square foot office building in proximity to that old building would cost $30 million or $300 per square foot. A fast way to find out these values is to talk to contractors who have recently built buildings in your town. Talk to the brokers to determine the new construction cost.

Your next step is to figure out how much it would cost to renovate the building to like-new conditions. Maybe you don't need to rebuild the walls, but you have to replace the windows, roof, and elevator, add fiber internet, and remodel the bathrooms and HVAC components. A contractor should be able to give you an estimate of those costs. The costs to renovate and repair can range from almost nothing to tens of millions of dollars, depending on the current condition of the property. If the building has been renovated in the last five years, you might be able to spend very little on repairs and updates. Alternatively, if the building has sat vacant for forty years, you're likely looking at a considerable investment simply to make the building habitable again. You also need to factor in the cost of land, permits, and timing.

Let's assume you can buy the old building for $5 million, or $50 per square foot, and it will cost you another $5 million to fix it up. Your final cost would be $10 million, which is significantly below that $30 million new-construction cost. "Wow, that is a great deal. Why doesn't everyone do that?" you might ask.

Well, not so fast. We have determined that the building and remodel are under new-construction cost, but we don't know if it will actually make any money at that price.

INCOME POTENTIAL

The next variable that plays into valuations is a property's income potential: how much income can that particular building produce?

As I introduced in the previous chapter, income is usually measured as net operating income (NOI), which factors into the property's capitalization rate, also known as cap rate. The cap rate gives you the rate of return for a property and can serve as a good barometer for the quality of an investment.

Cap rate % = net operating income ÷ property asset value

To continue with our office example, consider an office building in that market that has recently sold for $7.1 million. Based on market conditions, this building is expected to bring in $500,000 in NOI the following year. When we plug these numbers into the equation, we get a cap rate of 7 percent, also called a seven cap.

Now imagine that the market changes. The supply in the area has gone up, and office buildings in that market are now trading at an eight cap rate, which actually reduces the value. The office building is still bringing in the same income, and by rearranging the equation, we can use this new information to find the updated valuation in line with the market:

(NOI) ÷ cap rate = property asset value

($500,000) ÷ 8% = $6,250,000

It's the same building with the same income, but because the market changed the cap rate, the building's value decreased by almost $1 million. Nothing has changed other than the market determining that the valuation of that asset class has risen from a seven cap rate to an eight cap rate. As you can see, pricing can vary significantly depending on how the market is currently trading that particular asset class.

To continue our office evaluation, we know our fixed-up old building will cost us $10 million in cost, and we believe that an 8 percent cap rate is the market rate given the recession and decline in values overall. Our old building would need to be able to generate at least $800,000 in NOI to be worth $10 million. However, our goal is not to break even at $10 million in value. We would likely want to see potential NOI over $1 million to $1.1 million, giving our building a value of $12.5 million to $13.75 million at the current market 8 percent cap rate. Now, depending on your timing and hold period, you might build into your model the cap rate "compressing" and going back down to a 7 percent cap rate in a healthy market. This would make our old building worth NOI $1 million divided by a 7 percent cap, which equals $14.285 million with our $1 million in NOI at exit.

CONVERTING USE

Another strong value influencer is the building's use. Is it currently used as a hotel, office building, storage facility, or other? Often, you can get a significant discount on a property or add value by converting a building to a different use.

For example, if office buildings currently trade at an 8 percent cap rate in your chosen market, an office building that produces $400,000 in annual income will be worth $5 million. As part of your due diligence, you see that apartment buildings in the same market are trading for 5 percent cap rates, and maybe you purchase the building and convert it to apartments. Even if the apartment building brings in the same annual income, $400,000, its value will increase to $8 million because the market currently values apartment buildings more than office buildings. In this scenario, it would be worth it to convert the building to apartments as long as the conversion didn't cost you the $3 million difference in value.

To get the most value from your investment property, you'll want to study the market and determine the best use based on the cap rate for each asset class.

Let's say we look at that old office building and know it will cost us $10 million, but we determined that the office-building supply is quite abundant. The odds of filling up that building and hitting our $1 million in NOI would be a challenge even if it had a modern remodel, given that the market is just too saturated with office products. We could instead evaluate converting it to a multifamily building. When you want to change uses, the process often involves architects, engineers, and a contractor because the demand for the building will likely cause unknown changes.

For instance, the plumbing demand for an office building is not that significant. The building needs a handful of breakrooms and a couple of bathrooms per floor. Now think about a residential plumbing load. You have showers, baths, washing machines, dishwashers, and everyday water needs. That old building may need all new plumbing lines and larger city connections to satisfy that change of use.

For the sake of our example, let's assume that to convert from office to multifamily costs $8 million versus $5 million for an office modernization. However, we determine that we believe it is much more likely that we can achieve our $1 million NOI as an apartment building because there are limited supply and large demand. But our building and remodel have increased to $13 million in cost. Is it a good deal?

The good news is that we have a market cap rate of 5 percent, so $1 million in NOI means our stabilized multifamily project would be worth NOI $1 million divided by a 5 percent cap rate, which equals $20 million. I'd venture to say that it would be worth the extra remodel cost to increase the value to $20 million.

VALUATIONS DURING A RECESSION

Valuating properties can be fairly straightforward when you have access to all the data. However, this gets challenging during recessions when you might not be able to acquire information about a building. If a building goes into foreclosure, it might simply be impossible to get the data you want from the current owner. This is when investors tend to get scared away from deals; they aren't willing to take the risk of buying a building without information such as income and current condition.

Before you write off deals with less-than-complete information, there are a few assumptions you can make. One, during times of distress, the current income will not reflect typical income for the property. If the building from our previous example goes into foreclosure, we can assume it's no longer bringing in $400,000 a year. The owner didn't wake up one day and decide to stop paying their mortgage, despite having an income of nearly half a million dollars. No, something is driving the distress, whether it's tenants moving out, a market-wide shutdown like we saw with COVID-19, or some other recessionary event.

In this case, you don't *need* to know the building's current income because it won't give you useful information. For example, if you looked at the income of a hotel during a travel shutdown, it would tell you that the building was worth nothing. If travel stopped forever, this might be useful data, but you can probably assume that in a year or two, travel will slowly return to normal. In other words, if the whole market is experiencing distress, you can reasonably assume that the problem is not this particular property and the recession will eventually pass. Depending on the specific causes of the recession, you might also be able to assume that the building's income will return to its regular rate after the market recovers. Therefore, during a recession, it's much more useful to look at a building's past income rather than its current income.

Collect information on the building's past income and then try to determine how long it will take for the market to return to those conditions. During that time, you might choose to fix the property or simply hold it. You can make a profit by doing nothing more than waiting for the market to correct itself if you bought at a discount. During recessions, this shouldn't be difficult—you'll find many opportunities to invest in properties that produce cash flow but require little work because you're willing to move in a time of uncertainty. That said, you'll find the biggest discounts on properties that need a bit of elbow grease. Something happened to them—they stood vacant, the owners fell behind on maintenance, or some other happenstance—and now you need to clean them up or reposition them to boost their value.

KNOW YOUR MARKET

As a word of caution, past value and income will *often* indicate a property's post-recession potential, but this is not a strict rule. Understanding the market's trajectory will help you determine whether you can reach out and grab the knife, or whether it will only cut you on the way down.

Sometimes a recession is not a temporary period of distress but a seismic shift in the market. Consider Detroit, Michigan, which still has not fully recovered from the auto industry moving out of the market in the 1950s. That's not to say potential investment opportunities don't exist in places like Detroit. I have made great profits in that market by understanding where the fringes of opportunity were and where values might take longer to recover. Work to understand a market's movement and buy accordingly.

Picture a building in Detroit that's worth $10 million today but will decline to $9 million a year from now. If you can buy it for enough of a discount—let's say the owner is selling it for $5 million because it's going into foreclosure and they want to get rid of it quickly—and you turn around and sell it for $9 million next year, you can still make a profit. As long as the numbers work out in your favor, you can profit in almost any market.

When a market is declining—and if you determine that your exit plan is to sell while the market is still declining—then your plan is very time sensitive. Meaning the longer you hold on to the property, the less value it has since the market is declining. If you determine that the market is losing $1 million a year in value and you have $1 million a year in carrying cost, then you have a short time period to sell that building before you are upside down and losing money.

SEEK INSIGHTS FROM EXPERTS

Valuating properties might sound overwhelming at first, but as I'll cover in a future chapter, you don't have to manage it alone. An important part of investing is building a team of experts around yourself, and several key members of that team include a broker, appraiser, contractor, and lender.

Each of these professionals will have a specific insight into your market and can help you determine cap rates, typical property values, the cost to fix a property, and more. You don't need to know the finer details of every part of a valuation—and honestly, no single person can be an expert in everything—but it pays to have a solid high-level understanding of the mechanisms at work so you can look at a property and broadly answer the question, "Is this a good deal or not?"

In a declining market, be able to price in the market trajectory and decide whether it's worth reaching out and catching that knife. Sometimes it won't be—it all depends on how the numbers add up.

BREAKING DOWN A DEAL

At the end of the day, commercial real estate investing is all about math. Whether a deal is worth pursuing comes down to one question: Do the numbers add up in your favor? As Sam Zell stated at the start of this chapter, it all comes down to the bottom line.

A back-of-the-envelope analysis is the fastest and best way to determine if you should continue to dig deeper. The equation looks like this:

Property value (after-repair value) – cost of purchasing – cost of fixing the property – transactional costs = potential profit (or loss) on the deal

If you had a property worth $9 million after repairs that cost $5 million with $3 million in repairs and a 10 percent transactional cost, here's what you'd have leftover in profit:

$9 million – $5 million – $3 million – (0.1 × $9 million) = $100,000 potential profit

Is this a good deal? I don't think so. You're investing $8 million to make $100,000, which is only a 1.25 percent ROI. That is assuming an all-cash purchase. But if you were to utilize leverage, your equity investment amount would be lower, but your profit would be less. A good rule of thumb that I use and recommend is that you should look at your "all-in cost" to be 75 percent of the future value.

For this property, that would mean the target purchase price would be under $3.75 million. A purchase price of $3.75 million plus a $3 million remodel equals $6.75 million, or 75 percent of $9 million ARV.

$9 million – $3.75 million – $3 million – (0.1 × $9 million) = $1.35 million potential profit

That 75 percent of the future value gives you a margin of safety. It also gives you an exit strategy to refinance and pull out all your investment and keep a passive-income-producing property. But based on your financial goals and risk tolerance, you should decide your own cutoff for what the ROI should be before you give yourself the green light to do a deal. You'll also likely want to utilize a team approach—this does not need to be an individual journey. You can and should build a team to help you in this process.

If you don't have a team of experts yet, you can still start analyzing properties by using the tools I have provided on the resources page online. Plus, we are living in a world of abundant information, and you can spend hours, months, and years studying all the different asset classes that allow you to input the relevant data. Although these resources are not as accurate as a valuation reached by experts with a careful look at all the details, these online tools can give you a back-of-the-envelope calculation that will help you with a quick "go, no go" at a deal's potential.

That first look can often give you enough of an analysis to answer the question, "Should I dig deeper?"

Deep due diligence can involve weeks or months of gathering information, doing paperwork, and contacting the necessary people. Plus, proper due diligence costs money. It is not uncommon to spend several hundred thousands of dollars in due diligence reports, assessments, and evaluations. That is why using the quick back-of-the-envelope calculation helps you determine whether it is even worth investing money into proper due diligence.

Additionally, remember, time is your most valuable asset, and you shouldn't waste it on deals that don't fit your personal investment criteria. I have seen many investors sink hundreds of thousands of dollars into due diligence and discover significant issues with the property. If they are not able to reduce the purchase price accordingly, they should walk away. But the reality is that I have seen novice (and even professional) investors refuse to walk away from a deal because of their sunk due-diligence costs, and they buy a bad deal. This is further highlighted during periods of distress, when you must move quickly because the clock is ticking—you don't want to get stuck in a bad deal that sets you up for failure, especially when your whole goal is to buy at a discount before the market corrects—so it's critical to have your investment strategy in place and be able to act decisively.

SET YOUR OWN STANDARDS

You might still be wondering, *But what counts as a good deal?* The honest answer is that it depends on the criteria you've established for yourself. Each person's financial goals are different. If your goal is to slowly accrue money for earlier retirement, you might be satisfied with low-risk, low-reward deals, whereas someone willing to risk it all to retire by thirty-five might need a much higher ROI to consider a deal "worth it."

However, for everybody, a deal is no good if the numbers don't add up in your favor and end in a profit, which is why it's so important to understand your property valuations. If you can accurately evaluate deals, you'll have the confidence necessary to reach out and catch falling knives. Is reaching for that knife still going to be scary?

Absolutely. There will always be risks, and the next recession could come out of nowhere. An investment could outperform the market, or it could underperform, even if it looks good on paper. But by creating systems to judge deals, you'll have the level of comfort you need to make a decision, which is more than most people have during recessions. Once again, most people will be too afraid to act in times of distress, and therein lies your greatest opportunity.

TIPS AND TAKEAWAYS: WHAT'S A PROPERTY WORTH?

- Valuations take into consideration several variables, including the property's condition and repair costs, the building's replacement value, the location and land value, the property's income potential, and the building's current use.

- Recessions can make it difficult to acquire all the data you want about a property, but it's not always necessary to have current numbers. You can often tell more about a property's profit potential by looking at the building's past income than its current, recession-level income.
- To calculate your potential profit on a deal, use the following equation: Profit = property value – the cost of purchasing – the cost of fixing the property – transactional costs.
- It's critical to know the trajectory of your market so you can estimate if and when prices will correct. Sometimes a decline isn't a recession but a seismic shift in a market that can take decades to resolve.
- A lot of data goes into an accurate property valuation, but you don't need to handle it alone. You'll want to assemble a group of experts around yourself who can help you make good judgment calls about the deals you pursue or reject.
- At the end of the day, the only objectively bad deals are the ones that lose money or earn you such a small profit that they're a waste of time. Otherwise, as long as the risk, effort involved, and ROI of a particular deal fit your personal criteria and investing goals, it can be a good deal for you.

CHAPTER FIVE

GOING ONCE, GOING TWICE, SOLD

I was dancing on the skeletons of other people's mistakes.

—SAM ZELL

Sam Zell, also known as "The Grave Dancer," is a billionaire real estate investor, contrarian, and maverick. You may have noticed that I referenced some of his quotes a few times already, and that's because he is one of the more famous real estate investors who has been doing distressed investing for decades, and he's someone I have followed. You might also remember from the Introduction that I happened to be doing value-add work and fixing up office buildings for Equity Office Properties (EOP) at the start of my career. That was Sam Zell's office REIT that Blackstone bought at the peak valuation in 2007. I was too unaware to realize it at the time, but looking back now, I can see how some of those experiences have shaped my investment career today. As his nickname would indicate, Zell was known for buying things after people's mistakes and thus leads us up to the death of a deal: foreclosure.

In a recession, foreclosures are the inevitable ending point of the direst commercial real estate projects. They're the bellwethers of a changing market and one of the first signs of economic distress. As an investor, they're also your greatest opportunity to buy.

To find the best deals, it's critical that you understand the mechanisms of the foreclosure process so you know where to look and when to act. You want to be able to answer the question, "Where do I find the best-distressed opportunity pre-foreclosure, foreclosure, and post-foreclosure, aka real estate owned?" Also, "Where am I going to play in the capital stack?" meaning maybe you don't want to own the asset at all. You can just buy the note on the building. As the mortgage holder, you don't have to deal with things like fixing up the building or managing it. But maybe if the owner is not paying the mortgage, then you might foreclose on the property at a discount. Understanding the foreclosure process helps you better understand where you want to be when an opportunity presents itself.

Whether you plan to be an equity investor, be part of a fund that owns many buildings, buy the note on the property, or work some kind of creative structure, there will be different pros and cons to each element of the deal. You'll want to insert yourself in the foreclosure process earlier or later depending on your means and goals.

However, we'll start with, perhaps, the hardest part of the foreclosure process, which will set the stage for your success: finding available properties.

WHERE CAN YOU FIND FORECLOSED PROPERTIES?

Finding foreclosed (or soon-to-be foreclosed) properties isn't always as easy as looking at a directory. Sometimes you need to hunt for these deals, which means knowing where to look.

PUBLIC FORECLOSURE NOTICES

First, check the resource that is the closest you can get to a simple directory: public notices.

Lenders (banks) have legal requirements dictating a specific process they must follow when selling a foreclosed property. Each state is slightly different (between judicial and nonjudicial and the timing of the foreclosure process), but all of them involve a key part of that process, which is posting public notices letting people know where and when a property auction will take place. These public notices can reveal properties you might not have learned about otherwise because they're posted by the note holder, not the property owner.

"But if an owner can no longer afford a piece of property," you might ask, "why wouldn't they try to sell it themselves?"

Often, property owners who fall on hard times feel ashamed of their situations. Like ostriches burying their heads in the sand, many will try to hide their circumstances and avoid dealing with the problem for as long as possible. That means there might be properties in your target market that will be foreclosed on soon, but you won't see them listed in traditional ways such as CoStar, LoopNet, Crexi, or MLS sources—you need to check the public notices.

If you learn about a property in distress, you can reach out to the owner directly and come to an agreement with them. I have found that some owners are willing to sell to you for a discount because their alternative is going into foreclosure and losing everything. They might, in fact, be eager to get rid of the property. As someone who has been on both sides of the foreclosure process, I can very much understand the emotions. As a property owner, it is incredibly stressful to have creditors and people calling you up. You have tenants not paying rent, and your credit and financial situation is strained. As a buyer, if you can offer these owners a lifeline and a way to rid them of that stressful situation, it can be incredibly profitable for you.

To find public notices, simply google "public notices real estate" and the name of your market. Often, you can subscribe to a local newspaper or publication to get alerts when legal processes in the area have started. You can always access public notices for free, but that requires checking the local listing for that particular market every day. You'll have to manually scan through county recorder's office websites and other regional resources, which can throw so much information at you that it feels like drinking from a fire hose.

To make the process of tracking down foreclosure information easier, I suggest using a paid subscription service such as Roddy Report in Texas (**FLSonline.com**) or **propertyradar.com** in the western United States, to name a few. These technology platforms have truly disrupted the real estate space since their creation. They use APIs, algorithms, and other things that I don't fully understand to scrape and filter the data so you aren't wasting time reading through irrelevant newspaper ads and posts. You'll benefit the most from these services if you cast a wide net and monitor several markets at once. CoStar has recently purchased **Ten-X.com**, and you can also look at **Auction.com, Crexi.com**, and others for auction information. You can get a more comprehensive list on the resources page (**www.catchknives.com/resources**).

BUYING DISCOUNTED NOTES

Another strategy for finding properties in the foreclosure process is to work directly with banks. Due to regulations set by Dodd-Frank, defaulted, subperforming, or nonperforming loans are enormous red flags for their entities. Unpaid debts become highly detrimental to the lending bank because the bank now has to put up more cash as collateral for the nonperforming loan. In other words, when a loan is performing, regulators require the bank to have only a small percentage of the money held in reserve for that loan. When a loan is nonperforming, regulators require much more cash on hand to back the loan. In essence, a margin call on the bank.

What does this mean for you as a commercial real estate investor? This is one of the earliest places where an investor can insert themselves into a deal. We talked about the question "Where do you play in the capital stack?" This can be investing in the secured lender's position at a discount.

Why at a discount? Well, banks don't want to have to put up the extra collateral required for nonperforming loans, so they will often try to unload the loan as quickly as possible. They simply want to get it off their books. If that loan is backed by property, that means the bank will often sell the note (mortgage) for much lower than the unpaid balance (UPB) that you could normally find. Many new investors do not realize that the lender or bank that originates the loan is not necessarily the note holder. If you have ever signed a mortgage from your local bank and then sometime later you received a notice saying you need to make the payment to someone else, you may have experienced the bank selling the note. It's common for banks and lenders to sell pools of notes to other investors. In a recession, when it's likely that many loans are going into default at the same time, the discount you can get is even higher—you'll pay as little as forty, thirty, or even twenty cents on the dollar.

If you've read the book *The Big Short* by Michael Lewis or seen the subsequent movie, you may have some understanding of how those investors were shorting the underlying pools of bundled mortgages. I'm talking about buying some of those bad loans directly.

To see why a property might end up going into foreclosure and be sold at a huge discount, let's examine a few situations. Consider a $10 million note (mortgage) on a property that's currently worth only $8 million. No one's ever going to buy that mortgage for the full $10 million because it's more than the current value. You might, however, be able to buy it for a discount. Maybe there's defaulted interest, which has triggered the owner's financial issues, and now the bank has this mortgage weighing on their portfolio.

Keep in mind that banks follow certain regulations that make them behave in predictable ways. They look at their massive portfolios of mortgages and see a spreadsheet of numbers. Many banks group their mortgages either into a certain location or an asset type—they choose a niche and become experts in it—and when that asset type gets hit by a recession, it affects a huge percentage of their portfolio. To salvage what they can for their investors, they're more motivated to take a discount than a property owner might be.

How much of a discount you receive depends on many factors, including the following:

- The laws in your jurisdiction
- The current status of the property
- The status of the borrower
- Whether the borrower has other holdings
- Whether the borrower has a personal guarantee against the loan
- If they have recourse or not
- The value of the asset

Banks are willing to take the loss because by quickly selling the mortgage, they recoup at least some amount of money, and they can focus on their other, better-performing investments.

CASE STUDY: HOTEL NIGHTMARE OR DREAM?

In early 2020, COVID-19 travel lockdowns sent tourism into the dumps. The hotel industry had seen nothing like it ever before. Across the world, occupancy dropped from record highs of 60–70 percent to record unheard of lows of 0–5 percent. This was the straw that broke the camel's back for one hotel owner in Coachella Valley, California. They had recently built a 200-key, limited-service hotel in 2017. The developer spent $38 million, or $190,000 per key, building it and had a first mortgage with an unpaid balance of $20 million ($100,000 per key) and a healthy 53 percent LTC.

Here is where the deal starts to get a little interesting. The most recent 2019 appraisal note, which was BC (Before COVID) when the market was quite healthy, showed that the appraisal valued the project at $30 million. You might say, "But they just built the hotel for $38 million. How could the hotel be appraised for $30 million two years after opening?"

The answer is that they overbuilt the project, built too many rooms, and did too nice of a build-out for the area. Add in the equation that there was more supply that had recently been delivered, making room rates lower than they were expecting, and they had a problem. In early 2020, the lender who had the $20 million mortgage on the property was experiencing their own levels of distress as they saw multiple lines of business shut down all at once and they were getting margin called from their lenders.

In short, they were anxious to get rid of this hotel note in a hurry. So they sold the mortgage for $13 million. Now, the investor group doesn't own the hotel, just the mortgage on the property. But they had a significantly advantaged debt position if they had to foreclose on the property. Their exit strategy was either the borrower pays them as expected and they get paid off in full for the $20 million, or if they foreclose and then own the hotel, they own a $30 million property for $13 million plus some legal fees. All of that with no work, no remodel, and very limited operations, unless they chose to take over the property. That owner could even do a deed in lieu and save them the trouble of foreclosing and save his credit. For that owner, this property might have been a nightmare, but for those investors, I'd venture to say it was quite a dream. It just depends on the perspective from which you are looking at the deal.

MATURE MORTGAGES

To find properties of interest, you can also use subscription services to let you know when loans mature in your target market. In residential real estate, mortgages often span fifteen or thirty years, but commercial real estate mortgages mature much quicker. It's common for mortgages to be only two, three, five, or maybe ten years in duration, with very few lasting longer than a decade.

The opportunity for you as a distressed investment hunter lies in the scenario where an owner has a maturing loan or bridge loan as the market enters a down period. That owner already faces potential trouble because they have no option to refinance given the market value decline. They may face the situation needing to come out of pocket or pour more money into the project. It's possible that the value of their property has fallen so much that they now owe more on the mortgage than the property is worth. Naturally, that's a stressful situation, and many owners just want to wash their hands of the obligation.

At that point, they're often willing to sell at a discount to avoid losing money and going through the foreclosure process. So let's use an example of that hotel owner in the previous case study. That owner is facing the prospect of foreclosure, and he can put more money into the project (aka throw good money after bad), or he can bury his head in the sand and hope the problem goes away. Or maybe he accepts that he is going to lose money and is willing to get some amount of money out of the deal, so he is willing to sell the property at $21 million. You could step into the deal and now be the owner of that project, a $30 million hotel, for only $21 million. That's not a bad deal, but would you rather be the note holder or the person buying it directly from the owner? That all depends on your skills, your risk profile, and your ability to source deals.

CONTACTING OWNERS

If you intend to work directly with a property owner to buy their building, you can reach out to them in several ways: send them a letter, arrange a meeting in person, call them on the phone, or send them an email. This is another way in which technology has greatly expanded the ability to connect with property owners.

With residential real estate, you're often able to find the owner's contact information online or in county records, or simply run into them in person. Do you want to buy Joe Smith's house? Knock on his door and tell him. However, in commercial real estate, people tend to be more sophisticated about how they attach their identity to their purchases. The owner may be obscured behind a shell company or LLC, in which case, you might have to navigate a bit before you find their contact information.

Similarly, you usually can't hang out next to their property and wait for them to come by. I've owned commercial properties that I've hardly been to in person, so if you were to stand outside the office building I own in Milwaukee, you'd be waiting a long time, as I have been there only twice in four years. It's common for owners to not live in the same town, let alone the same state, as the property you're interested in buying.

Ideally, you don't want to have to track someone down and convince them to sell to you—you want to find motivated sellers who *want* to sell and will offer discounts or other incentives to make the buying process better for you. Sending out mailers, phoning property owners, or creating online outreach campaigns can all be effective ways to locate motivated sellers. With outreach activities, you won't have to waste time hunting for motivated sellers—they'll come to you.

Working directly with owners is one area I believe commercial real estate stands head and shoulders above other investment types. Consider the stock market, where you can go to prison for insider trading—just look at Martha Stewart. It's against the law to use insider knowledge to guide your investment decisions. In contrast, gaining insider knowledge in real estate is encouraged. You *should* be communicating with property owners and other parties to find out if they're willing to sign a deed in lieu of foreclosure, to agree on creative financing solutions, and to give you knowledge that lets you make a more accurate property valuation. The more you know, the more you can arrange a deal that plays in your favor.

THE FORECLOSURE PROCESS

Now that you know where to find foreclosures in your market, it also helps to understand what happens during the foreclosure process itself. Depending on your goals and circumstances, you might choose to insert yourself into the process at different stages. For example, if you wanted to work out a deal directly with the owner, you might contact them after the notice of sale goes out but before the auction. If you'd prefer not to work with the owner, you could wait and attend the auction in person.

STAGE ONE: THE BORROWER DEFAULTS ON PAYMENTS

The foreclosure process first gets triggered when a borrower falls behind on paying their mortgage. A lender can choose to initiate the foreclosure process immediately, or they can offer a grace period in which the borrower can pay the debt along with a late fee.

STAGE TWO: NOTICE OF DEFAULT

If a certain amount of time passes with no payment (laws vary by state, but this period is frequently ninety days), the lender sends a notice of default. The notice states the balance due and tells the borrower that if they do not pay their debt by a set date, there will be a notice of sale for the property.

STAGE THREE: NOTICE OF SALE

If the borrower still hasn't paid, the process moves to stage three, the notice of sale. The notice states the date on which the property will be sold at a public auction. Different jurisdictions will have different rules requiring a set amount of time between the notice and the auction; this period is usually thirty, sixty, or ninety days.

STAGE FOUR: AUCTION

After the dictated period between the notice of sale and the date of the auction arrives, the auction takes place on the courthouse steps or another public venue. The auction crier typically reads the legal description of the property and may give purported addresses. They announce the opening bid established by the bank and then take bids from attendees. As a buyer, you bid on the mortgage in person. If you make the winning bid, most states require you to pay in cash, cashier's check, or other certified funds for the amount you bid. Other states may require only a deposit on the day of the auction, followed by the rest of the funds wired within twenty-four hours.

STAGE FIVE: NEW OWNERSHIP

At this point, you technically own that mortgage, which has gone through the foreclosure process. You may need to change the locks or otherwise remove people from the property. If the building is an apartment building, retail center, or other tenant property, you'll also want to contact those tenants and notify them that you're the new owner and they should now pay rent to you. Also, depending on locale or the lease terms, sometimes those commercial leases do not carry over to the new owner as a foreclosure causes default provisions from the owner's position. This could be problematic. If tenants all of a sudden no longer have valid leases, they could just move out whenever they want and leave you with an empty building. Getting those leases will sometimes be hard in a foreclosure process since no one is brokering the deal.

DOWNSIDES OF FORECLOSURE

As the buyer, foreclosure can get you steep discounts, but it also comes with downsides. First, as a legal process, foreclosure can be cumbersome and time consuming. Depending on the state and jurisdiction and whether the process is judicial or nonjudicial, foreclosure can take anywhere from six months to several years to resolve. At that time, you might buy the note and still not control the property. The owner would stay in control until the foreclosure process has ended. In that hotel case study, the owner could just not pay their mortgage, and the new investors who bought it for $13 million would not get any payments. In California, that legal process to foreclosure could run many months and well into years.

You can earn fantastic returns by buying at thirty cents on the dollar, but imagine that it takes two years to foreclose. In those two years, a lot can happen to lower the value of your investment: the property's condition can worsen, tenants can move out, the market can change. When you bought the note, the property, perhaps, had a value of $10 million. Now, by the time you take control of it, it's worth only $8 million. These are risks you need to consider when dealing with a property at any stage of the foreclosure process.

As I mentioned before, you can sometimes avoid the fore-closure process by directly reaching out to the owner or bank *before* the property goes into foreclosure. Sometimes, however, it is unavoidable. For example, if properties have been pooled together, there's often no way to work out a transfer without the notes going through the foreclosure process. Another scenario where foreclosure is unavoidable is when the owner does not respond to outreach (remember, it's not unusual for distressed owners to bury their heads in the sand) or they've died and nobody has taken over their estate. There's nobody to resolve the defaulted loan outside of the foreclosure process.

In these situations, you need to accept foreclosure as part of the deal and account for the costs in time, money, and effort when working through your profit equation.

WHEN SHOULD YOU GET INVOLVED IN A FORECLOSURE?

Now that you have a loose overview of the foreclosure sequence of events, let's say that you see a public notice announcing that a mortgage on a property has gone into default. At what point do you get involved? How do you make that decision?

There are pros and cons to getting involved immediately as a buyer versus waiting for the auction itself.

Getting Involved Early in the Foreclosure Process

Pro: Less Competition

One advantage of contacting the owner or bank early in the foreclosure process is that you'll have less competition for the property. At the public auction, anybody can show up and outbid you on the spot. However, if you get involved early enough, you might be the only investor talking to the owner. They might decide to sell to you to quickly resolve their situation without any competing investors weighing in at all.

Pro: More Control over the Price You Pay

In commercial real estate, properties with positive equity in them (the property's market value is higher than the amount owed on the mortgage) rarely make it to auction. Consider a property worth $15 million with a mortgage for only $10 million—that property has $5 million in equity. It would be foolish for the owner to let the property go to auction instead of trying to sell that mortgage for $12 million or $13 million earlier in the process. This scenario presents a great opportunity to work with the current owner and come up with a price that benefits you both. Many owners will choose to go this route to avoid the lengthy and cumbersome foreclosure process. You retain the bargaining power you would lose in a public auction and still have the chance to buy the property for significantly less than it's worth.

Con: You might have to negotiate with the current owner

Negotiating with the current property owner can be a pro or a con, depending on the person. If you're unlucky, the owner will make the process more difficult. If the property lost value since they bought it, they might be biased and fixated on the original price. There also might be a sentimental attachment to the property, for example, if it housed their family's restaurant business for years. Owners can have many reasons for not seeing the true market value of their property, which can make negotiations hard.

Waiting for the Auction

Pro: No negotiation with the current owner

As I described above, one pro of waiting for the auction is that you don't have to negotiate with the current owner about what they think is a fair price. At the auction, you pay only as much as the bidding demands with no hang-ups or complications.

Con: Few deals make it this far

Relatively few properties make it all the way through the foreclosure process, so if you've waited this long, you've probably missed out on some of the better deals. Technology has disrupted the foreclosure process, allowing more people to see public notices and act on deals sooner by working directly with owners and banks. In an auction, you're more likely to see securities that are equal to or more than the value of the properties; you'll see few properties that have equity in them.

COMPETING IN YOUR IDEAL WINDOW

As I've mentioned several times throughout the book, technology has disrupted the real estate world and made it more accessible than ever. You no longer need to have an office in every market to be able to find and capitalize on their deals. With this in mind, you might be wondering, *How can I get the best deals when I'm competing with other investors from around the world?*

There are three reasons this isn't as serious a problem as it sounds. The first is that despite being accessible to people from all over the world, commercial real estate investing actually involves quite a small community. Compared to other types of investing, not many people buy commercial properties; in major cities, perhaps four or five families control most of the deals (remember the "mafia rule"). When you consider the top fifty cities in the United States, that's a group of only about 250 people who are looking at relevant property information.

The second reason you shouldn't be too concerned about

competition is that the pool gets even smaller when you focus on deals between $2 million and $25 million. In that sweet spot, deals will be just out of range of your average mom-and-pop investor, but they'll also be too small to be noticed by large, institutional investors. Every deal involves roughly the same amount of work, so why would a large investor bother making 10 percent on a $10 million deal when they could spend the same amount of time making 10 percent on a $100 million deal?

They wouldn't, and these institutional investors, such as Blackstone and Colony Capital, make up approximately 80 percent of the commercial real estate world. They collectively wield trillions of dollars, so you wouldn't want to compete with them. Simply by staying under their radar in the $2 million to $25 million range, you eliminate most of the commercial real estate competition.

You can further thin out your competition by focusing on smaller cities—secondary and tertiary markets—instead of large core markets such as San Francisco, Seattle, Los Angeles, Miami, New York, and Chicago, which have a ton of wealthy investors. In smaller cities, there might be only four other people looking at deals in your range. The downside is that by definition, secondary and tertiary cities are smaller. That means you'll find fewer opportunities for investing: there are fewer office buildings, fewer shopping centers, fewer everything. By going into these markets, you're trading more deals for less competition.

The third reason to not be overly concerned about competition is this: You *can* invest in properties from anywhere in the world, but there are still benefits to investing in the market where you live. This especially applies to physically distressed properties that need a lot of rehab work. If you are coordinating with contractors and inspectors, you'll want to have boots on the ground to make sure the project stays on track. So if a hotel in your market needs a massive renovation, much of the remote competition will likely eliminate itself due to location and proximity to the property. You may not have to compete with every investor in the world, just the ones in your local market.

Without systems in place to manage remote purchasing, it can be challenging to invest in secondary and tertiary markets if you don't live in one, even if you aren't focusing on highly distressed properties. Consider this: If you're based in Los Angeles, you can easily develop a network of brokers in the city, get to know other investors there, and become more familiar with the market. Maybe there are more opportunities to invest in Boise, Idaho, at that moment, but those deals might be more difficult to manage than the property you can drive to in downtown LA every day.

No matter what you do or which market you invest in, there

will always be *some* competition and tradeoffs. However, timing also plays a factor in your success. Even well-funded people with wealth tend to go into preservation mode during recessions. They get what I call alligator arms, as they retract from their usual investment activity and choose to limit their risk. In general, as the market falls, you'll find fewer people actively looking for deals, which means less competition. Again, if you can get over your fear of uncertainty during recessionary times, you can make a fortune.

TIPS AND TAKEAWAYS: GOING ONCE, GOING TWICE, SOLD

- Foreclosures are excellent opportunities for investors because owners often want to sell quickly before the property goes to auction, and they are therefore willing to sell at a discount.
- You can find available foreclosures in your target market by searching public foreclosure notices, working directly with banks to purchase notes, finding mature mortgages during down periods, and contacting owners who might be willing to sell.
- The foreclosure process has five stages: defaulting on payments, a notice of default, notice of sale, auction, and new ownership.
- There are pros and cons to getting involved early in the foreclosure process—and working out a deal directly

with the current owner or lender—versus waiting until the property goes to public auction.

- To limit your competition, aim to operate within the $2 million to $25 million range. You'll avoid both low-level investors looking for cheaper properties and high-level institutional investors controlling the upper end of the market.
- Secondary and tertiary markets often have the best deals for mid-tier investors and less institutional competition.

CHAPTER SIX

ALMOST FREE: CREATIVE WAYS TO FINANCE YOUR PURCHASES

Ninety percent of all millionaires become so through owning real estate. More money has been made in real estate than in all industrial investments combined. The wise young man or wage earner of today invests his money in real estate.

—ANDREW CARNEGIE

As a commercial real estate investor, you can get the biggest discounts during recessions—but there's a catch. It's also harder to secure funding to finance your purchases during periods of distress than it would be during a thriving market. In other words, the deals are there, but the traditional financing sources are not.

WAYS TO PURCHASE PROPERTY

During the next downturn, you're likely to face this challenge as a new investor, which is why finding creative ways of financing should be the next tool on your investing tool belt. Even if you don't yet have a significant amount of cash to invest, by using creative financing options, you can still get in the real estate game and start building your portfolio.

CASH IS ALWAYS EASIEST

The easiest, most hassle-free way to purchase property will always be by paying cash. It takes the pain out of finding financing because there *is* no external financing. You don't need to work with lenders, go through approval processes, or jump through any other hoops because you're paying with your own money. That said, most people don't have $2 million, $5 million, or $10 million in cash sitting in their bank account. Paying cash might not be a viable option, so you'll want to look into other financing methods.

TRADITIONAL LENDERS

During a normal, healthy market, working with a traditional lender is the primary way most people buy commercial real estate. But in a recession, banks and other lenders react to the perceived increase in risk and, generally, lend less. Several things happen at once to make them hesitant to finance new purchases. One, they look at their own portfolios and see properties falling into distress or even foreclosure. Two, they're legally obligated to hold on to more cash as assets become distressed. And three, they see the falling market and feel uncertainty over when it will correct. As a cumulative effect, the banks decide to put strict limitations on what they'll lend, and you're left with the inability to use traditional financing.

Try to see the issue from their perspective. When a bank lends you money to buy a property, they don't enjoy the same upsides as you do if the deal works out. You benefit when you get a large discount and a significant profit, but all the bank gets is the interest on the loan. The best-case scenario is that you pay the loan as agreed upon. The worst case is they now have to take significant discounts, legal fees, and forgo years of payment and, ultimately, manage something that they are not in the business of managing. In fact, they get the interest whether or not the investment succeeds. They also have to deal with the risk of you not repaying your loan. In a recession, you potentially have a lot to gain by buying a property at that moment, but the bank would only get their normal amount of interest, with the added risk of you defaulting because of distress. In short, the bank has no potential for additional profits but shoulders the risk of losing the entire loan, so it's no wonder that they stop lending during recessions.

This lack of financing can be a challenge, but on the flip side, it also drives further discounts. If a property owner wants to sell quickly because their mortgage is going into foreclosure, they might choose to accept less than the property is worth due to a lack of options. Consider, if their property is worth $10 million, they might accept $7 million simply because, without traditional financing options, not many interested buyers have $10 million in cash at that time. They have to either take what buyers offer or hold on to the property longer. The fact that no one likes that investment at the time very much can play to your advantage. Remember, *you make your money when you buy it, and you try not to lose it while you remodel or hold it.*

NEGOTIATION

When I say "creative ways of financing," I genuinely mean creative. One of the commercial real estate's greatest strengths compared to other investment vehicles is that everything is up for negotiation. There's no limit to how creative you can get in structuring your deal, so you can create opportunities to transfer titles and ownership without ever utilizing a bank. Negotiations are also when you benefit the most from insider information about a property, the market, and the seller because you'll have a hint as to how you can best work the deal.

As an example, you might know that the seller is a doctor who owns a practice, and they're looking to sell their current property and lease one that's 20,000 square feet. If you own a 20,000 square foot property, you could arrange a highly favorable deal to buy the doctor's property for a discount and lease your property to them, all without putting any money into the deal. In this way, by working with multiple assets in combination or parallel, you can transfer ownership without any immediate financing.

If you don't have access to financing during a recession, think about what you *do* have. What assets do you own? You can likely leverage something in a creative way that will take the place of financing until the recession passes.

RETIREMENT FUNDS

Another creative option for financing a real estate purchase is to tap into a self-directed IRA or other retirement accounts. If you've been working in a career for decades, you might not have millions of dollars in cash in the bank, but perhaps you have significant funds in your retirement account. Using your retirement funds for real estate comes with some legal restrictions, so I recommend checking out *The Self-Directed IRA Handbook* by Mat Sorensen and consulting financial advisors or an attorney if you move forward with this option.

As a word of advice: Most financial advisors who manage your account typically make a portion of fees off you keeping your account invested with them. Even though they are supposed to be true fiduciaries and help you with advice, just remember, your retirement plan means a monthly paycheck to them. Often, they will tell you that you shouldn't be risky with your money.

Leveraging a self-directed IRA can not only be an effective way to buy real estate during a recession, but it can also be a wise use of those funds. During a period when the stock market is overvalued, you'll likely want to transfer some of your assets into another vehicle. With a self-directed IRA, you'd have the option to put some of those funds in a property, such as an office building, that you could lease out to generate passive income. In this way, you can invest in real estate without using a bank at all. Alternatively, a bank might lend but with lower levels of leverage, and your retirement account allows you to greatly expand your buying power.

SELLER FINANCING

To buy property in a recession, you might also consider seller financing. Imagine that you have a few million dollars and you want to buy an $8 million mortgage on a building that you know is actually worth $15 million. You might approach the current owner, who is falling behind on their mortgage payments, and say, "I'm willing to buy your building, but I don't have the total amount of money right now. Instead, I can give you $1 million now, and we'll leave the existing mortgage in place. I'll catch up the mortgage payments and assume your financing from here on out."

In effect, you're taking over the current owner's mortgage so you don't have to work with a bank to finance a new one. The current owner benefits because they no longer need to worry about defaulting and going into foreclosure; they can wash their hands of the property. You benefit by gaining control of the asset without needing to pay the total amount in cash up front or needing to work with a bank.

I already see some of you out there saying, "But WAIT! That's not true. You can't assume mortgages because they have due on sale clauses."

Yes, some mortgages are assumable outright. The bank typically charges a fee and wants to underwrite you, but the bank actually benefits because now someone is paying the mortgage. The insider tip is that when the mortgage is "reperforming," it no longer puts a red flag on their portfolio and it solves one of their immediate problems. Although, yes, due on sale clause provisions technically say that it prevents you from assuming them outright, understand that during recessions, banks aren't typically too concerned with who is paying the mortgage and how creditworthy they might be or not. They are primarily concerned that it is being paid. I have not seen a mortgage holder ever invoke a due on sale clause on a mortgage. I am not saying it doesn't happen, but when it does, it is mostly in good times and not when they are dealing with a mountain of distressed properties. Additionally, there are legal ways you can get around some of these restrictions by using LLCs or other advanced ownership legal tactics. I recommend consulting an attorney if you choose this option.

Also, I want to address the idea of no-money-down financing and explain why the title of this chapter includes the phrase "almost free." Some books will tell you how to purchase property with no money down—this is not that kind of book. In fact, I've found that by putting at least a little money down, you have more bargaining power, sellers are more willing to work with you on creative financing options, and you're more likely to get the deal done. Sellers become wary when they're asked to hand over their property with no money down. But like in the example above, if you offer the seller $1 million up front, that gives them enough money to pay off other debts, invest in a new project, or otherwise go off and do something else, leaving you to fix up their old property and make a profit on it.

In short, seller financing can get you excellent discounts and a deal for almost no money down. When an owner is exhausted and facing foreclosure, they frequently want to avoid further financial stress and not deal with the problem property anymore. When you come in with the energy to fix up the property and offer to assume their debt, it can be a win-win scenario for you both.

MASTER LEASE

A master lease is similar to seller financing in that you're assuming the existing debt. It differs, however, because you sign a master lease for the entire building with the option to buy and with the ability to sublet it for a higher amount of money. For example, you might sign a master lease with an option to buy a multifamily building and then rent out the rooms on Airbnb. You're paying little to nothing because the room-to-room rate you're charging on Airbnb—the rental income you're bringing in—pays for the lease you've signed. In commercial real estate, you might create a profitable arbitrage opportunity by signing a lease on a restaurant for cheap and renting it out as a ghost kitchen operator on a month-to-month basis.

The master lease approach allows you to control property with almost no money down—you may only need good credit to get approved on the lease, and often in distressed times, normal things like creditworthiness are thrown out.

It gives you time to control the asset and invest money into it with the goal of improving it to a target future value. It also allows you to immediately bring in income while lending markets correct and, eventually, come back online.

ALTERNATIVE (ASSET-BASED) LENDERS

You might also secure funds through alternative lenders, also known as hard money loans or private lenders. Alternative lenders can provide money quickly, with the major downside that they tend to charge much higher interest rates than traditional lenders. However, the upside is that after traditional lenders have gone underground during recessions, alternative lenders will still be there for you. They make loans based on the asset, not so much on the borrower.

You'd rather not pay a high-interest rate, of course, but if you have the opportunity to buy a property for pennies on the dollar, you can pay the alternative lender's interest and still make a fortune. You might purchase a building for only 30 percent of its worth and pay 15 percent for the loan, which still leaves you with a significant and healthy 55 percent potential profit margin. Like I've stressed throughout this book, whether something is a good deal all comes down to how the numbers add up. If a high-interest alternative lender is your only financing option, you can still make a fantastic profit if it's a good deal.

Understand, however, that many alternative lenders operate like typical sharks. They look at the world differently
than a bank would. Remember when I said banks think the
best-case scenario is that you pay the loan as agreed upon?
These alternative lenders think the opposite: the worst-case
scenario is that you pay the loan as agreed upon. They are
rooting for your success, but to be honest, they are underwriting the asset and would love for you to not execute
your plan properly or leave too thin a margin because if
you default on your loan, they can take over your equity
position. Let's say you're buying a $5 million property for
$3 million; you're using $1 million of your own money and
borrowing $2 million from an alternative lender. From the
lender's perspective, either they get paid the high interest
you owe them, or you default and they take ownership of
the property for $2 million. Either way, they win. The real
question is, will you win, too?

In summary, alternative lenders empower you to move
quickly and with less red tape, but always remember that
they're underwriting your loan with high interest and the
anticipation that you'll fail.

PARTNERSHIPS

Commercial real estate is a team sport. Few people possess
all the necessary skillsets and tools to complete the different tasks required to succeed. In this spirit, partnerships

are another viable way to creatively finance a purchase. Whom should you partner with? One of your best options is a contractor.

Needing a contractor involved in nearly everything you do in real estate is, perhaps, the most frustrating and maddening part of the entire process. But if you partner with a contractor to buy a property, you eliminate some of that pain. They bring one skillset to the table—how to build and fix a property in a cost-effective way—and you can bring another—funding, business acumen, connections, or any other skills you have.

Imagine that you have enough money to buy a heavily distressed property at a discount, but you won't have enough money to complete the necessary repairs. If you partner with a contractor, they may be willing to do the work at a lower profit margin or even at cost because they have equity in the deal. Contractors generally have healthy profit margins in good times. When markets slow down, they too typically slow down, and this can be an opportunity to create a win-win strategy, which can save you a significant amount of money.

You might find other people who would make beneficial partners; just think of who would balance your personal skillset and save you money.

CASE STUDY: MONEY IS A TOOL

I am going to tell you about one of those aha moments that was shared with me by a developer when I was a young and eager novice wanting to figure out which way was up. I am assuming you have seen the type of giant bulldozers and graders that do heavy, earth-moving construction. They're the tractors that my sons absolutely love and make us stop to look at from time to time because, let's be honest, those tractors are rad. They can literally move mountains, build roads, and prep for subdivisions and shopping centers.

Most people can also quickly guess that those machines cost millions of dollars. What most people don't know is that very few contractors own those machines. They're mostly owned by equipment companies such as Hertz or United Rentals, and they rent the machines on a daily, weekly, or monthly basis. The rental rate might be $2,000 per day, $10,000 a week, and $30,000 a month. A contractor will figure out how long they need to use the machine to move, say, 2,000 cubic yards of dirt, and then they'll rent the machine. They get to use a $1 million tractor for a month for $30,000. If they bid on the job properly, they might make $170,000 or more in profit. When people hear that, the business arrangement seems totally reasonable and like no big deal.

But if I were to tell you that I borrowed $1 million and paid $30,000 a month in payments, most people would think that's insane and way too risky. That is likely because most people are familiar with interest rates on their home loan, and something that isn't low single digits seems crazy. But if I could pay annually 36 percent interest for a month, but it allows me to make $170,000 or maybe more in profit, is that crazy?

The aha moment for me was that money is a tool, and you are renting the money just like a contractor rents an excavator to get a job done. You need the money to get a job done, and if used as a tool, you have to pay a daily or monthly rental rate to get the privilege to use that money. Although interest rates might eat up your profits, don't be as concerned with how much the "rent" is for your tool as you are concerned with what it means to the overall project's success.

WHOLESALING

Wholesaling represents another approach to commercial real estate where you can act as a middleman without putting your own money into a deal. As a wholesaler, you find properties to sell to investors. You do the work of negotiating a deal with the seller and then you turn around and resell the property to someone else. Best of all, you don't need to put your own money into the transaction. How does this work?

Imagine that you're a wholesaler and you know a doctor who owns multiple offices. He's always looking to expand his practice and will reliably pay $5 million for 50,000 square foot buildings. He's also extremely busy and doesn't want to spend his spare time searching for properties.

As a wholesaler, you would make it your goal to find a 50,000 square foot building and get it under contract for less than what the doctor will pay. You work with the seller and get the building under contract for $4 million, but you don't close on the property. You would, instead, immediately go to the doctor and tell him that you have a property he'd like, and you'll sell it to him for $5 million. He agrees, and in one fell swoop, you close both deals without needing to put your own money into the transaction. The seller walks away satisfied because they made $4 million. The doctor walks away satisfied because he bought a property that fits his criteria without having to do any of the work finding it. Last, you walk away with $1 million having worked as the middleman to facilitate the sale. Everyone wins.

As you can probably imagine, networking is crucial to wholesaling success. You'll be able to sell most consistently if you've built connections with investors and understand the type of assets they're looking to acquire. There are many books and strategies to get started as a wholesaler. It is by far one of the lowest-cost entry points to get into commercial real estate investing, as it mostly takes a lot of sweat equity and turning over rocks to find deals. If the deal is good enough, you won't have a hard time selling it for a profit or "assignment fee." As a new investor, most people don't know what a good deal is yet, so it's a bit of the blind leading the blind. But don't be discouraged. The more you learn, the more profitable this part of the business becomes. In time, you will see that it's much harder to find great deals than it is to find the money to buy the deal.

ACT AS A LENDER

The last category I'll discuss here is acting as a lender,

which isn't a way to finance your own property purchase but rather an alternative way to invest in commercial real estate. With this route, you're taking on the role of an alternative lender. You might lend another investor $2 million at 10–12 percent, for example. You don't own the property yourself; you lend money to someone else buying property and make money on the interest. You become the shark that lends people the money and doesn't have to do the hard work. Your tradeoff is a cap on your profits, but this is much easier for many busy professionals. I know several accredited investors whose preferred method of investing is acting as a lender. They put capital into a debt fund that pays out a fairly consistent monthly payment, and they get to avoid learning the ins and outs of every property or area they are lending on.

WHICH FINANCING OPTION SHOULD YOU CHOOSE?

As you now know, you have many options for buying commercial real estate outside of traditional lending. But which is the right choice for you?

Under the right circumstances, any of these financing options could result in massive success. But as I discussed in Chapter 3, you want to start any potential deal by deciding your exit strategy. What does the market trajectory look like? How long will you hold the property? Will it be difficult to sell? How much money will you have to spend fixing it up? Do you want to make money by collecting rent or by selling the property for more than you paid? Answer these questions and choose the financing option that best aligns with your overall strategy.

Also, weigh the pros and cons of each route. Consider the wholesaling example above—it ended in a $1 million profit with no money invested. The return on deals like that is infinite because you aren't limited by the cash in your bank account. There's also practically no risk. You are, however, limited by your time, which makes that deal difficult to replicate or scale. The same limitation applies to many of the other financing options in that they each require varying amounts of time and money.

When choosing how to finance your investment, you'll want to consider time and effort. For example, as a professional investor, I invest in up markets, down markets, and every market in between. I've built relationships with contractors over the years, and now those ongoing partnerships have grown fruitful with little ongoing work. But when you're just getting started, building relationships with the right partners takes a huge amount of time. You'll want to consider how the time commitment of each option will fit into your schedule, especially if you plan to continue working your regular job.

In general, catalog the assets you have at your disposal and decide what excites you. If you're a people person with some cash to invest, partnering with a contractor might be the perfect option for you. If you're short on cash but have a lot of time, maybe wholesaling would suit you better. If you don't have much liquidity but have a super-solid deal lined up, you might be able to earn a huge profit by working with an alternative lender. Or if you have the funds but you don't have the time, then finding an operator or a fund to invest into might be more up your alley. Think about what you have and use it to your advantage.

Several of these options involve not personally owning real estate, so you'll want to weigh the long-term pros and cons of that as well. For example, inflation will affect you more as a wholesaler, someone who doesn't own property and has all their net worth in cash, than an investor who has shifted some of their retirement funds into real estate. The benefit of owning real estate is that as inflation occurs and the value of the dollar falls, prices increase. A loaf of bread might rise in cost to $3, and similarly, your building that was worth $10 million when you bought it might now be valued at $15 million. Meanwhile, the buying power of the money in your bank account decreases. In this way, owning real estate protects you somewhat against the effects of inflation.

In late 2020 and early 2021, the Fed is still busy printing trillions—yes, trillions with a T—of stimulus funding. Every reserve bank on the planet is currently doing the same thing, and cryptocurrencies and stock markets are spiking to record highs with record low interest rates as well. Maybe you have heard the headline "Don't fight the Fed" or "Don't Bet against the US"? Those lines mean that the Fed is trying to inflate the market back up to normal trendlines. Study this topic, and you'll see that the Fed and their money printing is more like a train than a race car. Once that inflation gets rolling, it is hard to stop and could be setting us up in the near future for some significant inflation.

Let's not forget about death—or that other one, TAXES. You'll want to consider how your financing choices will impact your taxes. There's a reason many ultra-wealthy individuals pay almost nothing in taxes, and it's because tax laws favor people who own real estate. You'll especially benefit from this if you're a high-income individual because you can offset your income through capital gains, cost segregation, bonus depreciation, interest write-offs, and many more. Of course, by now you know to consult proper tax advisors. If you're wholesaling, you're missing out on the tax benefits that come from owning property yourself.

Last, always keep your sight on your idea of financial freedom. What will it take to live the lifestyle you want?

When you're a middleman, you make a quick buck, but you're still on a hamster wheel. After one deal is done, you need to move on to the next. If you own real estate, you can create passive income. You earn money while you sleep, and that income grows with every deal you complete. Lending is a bit of a hybrid of that. You make money while you sleep, but you have to redeploy when those loans are paid off. Consider as a long-term property holder that each property you add to your portfolio builds on the ones that came before it, whereas you don't get the same cumulative effect with wholesaling or with lending.

After what I just said, wholesaling and lending might sound unfavorable because you don't get the same level of write-offs and tax benefits, but remember, buying real estate comes with risks, too. For example, imagine that you sign a $3 million mortgage at 15 percent interest with a private lender. You plan on selling the property in three years, but then your plan goes sideways. Perhaps you're hit with cost and time overruns, and now that mortgage hits you like a freight train. Not only are you losing the time and money you've already put into the deal, but the lending company can come after you personally. When you structure a deal in this way, your risk profile can be much higher than if you had decided to invest via acting as a lender. The lender made more money than you did and didn't do any of the work.

Again, any of these financing options have the potential to grow your wealth, but I hope to steer you away from the more common mistakes you can make when you're getting started and show you your options. I don't want you to wind up sitting on a street curb praying to erase your debt like I found myself doing years ago. If my advice can save you from sleepless nights and help you be profitable, I've accomplished my goal, and hopefully, so have you.

TIPS AND TAKEAWAYS: CREATIVE WAYS TO FINANCE YOUR PURCHASES

- During recessions, traditional financing options tend to vanish, so to fund your real estate purchases, you may have to get creative.
- You have many different options for financing your purchase: negotiation, retirement funds, seller financing, master lease, alternative lenders, and partnerships.
- You can also choose to make money in ways that don't require owning property: wholesaling and acting as a lender.
- Any financing option can be profitable, but you'll want to choose the option that will be successful for your particular investment strategy. Consider your financial goals, exit strategy, risk tolerance, interests, skillset, and assets and decide which financing source best aligns with those criteria.

CHAPTER SEVEN

DON'T BUY THIS PROPERTY

If you don't look on yourself and think, "Wow, how stupid I was a year ago," then you must not have learned much in the last year.

—RAY DALIO

By this point in the investment process, you might be excited to buy. You know how to start the process of estimating the value of properties, find foreclosures, and finance your purchase. If you've found a distressed piece of commercial real estate that looks like a winner on paper, you might even be ready to make a deal.

But hold on. Sometimes, instead of pulling the trigger on a deal, you'd be much better off pulling the plug. There are red flags you need to look for that can reveal when a property seems too good to be true. Depending on the specifics, issues such as contamination, structural problems, deferred maintenance, back taxes, accessibility issues, and more can all make a property an unviable investment.

To succeed in this field, you'll have to spot these red flags, mitigate your risk by doing your due diligence, and know where to look for relevant information. Once you can recognize the warning signs of a bad deal, you'll see that some properties have so many problems that you could take possession for free and still lose money.

DOING YOUR DUE DILIGENCE

In every form of real estate purchasing or investment, due diligence plays a critical part in the exploration process. However, the distinction with distressed commercial real estate investing, where you need to act quickly to catch a falling knife, is that you often have to work with less information and in a smaller time frame. During a normal market, you might have thirty to sixty days for due diligence; with a distressed property, you'll usually have less. You might not have time to run as thorough an analysis as you would like. For buildings going through the foreclosure process, you might not even be able to get inside the building to assess the interior condition. So how are you supposed to judge a deal based on incomplete information?

The pressure of time and limited access make it all the more critical that distressed commercial real estate investors have a solid understanding of the due diligence process. First, realize that a distressed property, by its nature, will likely have problems. To find out how big those problems are, start by asking the following questions:

- Why are the current owners losing this property?
- Why is the property going to foreclosure?
- What is the distress? What's going wrong?
- Is the property losing income or decreasing in value?
- What are the macro elements confounding the situation? Is there a recession? A pandemic? Has a major employer left the city?

Understanding the nature of the foreclosure will help guide your due diligence process so you can uncover enough information to make a good decision.

WHERE TO LOOK FOR INFORMATION

You need to research a property, but where do you start the search?

First, I want to make it clear where you *shouldn't* start: with a real estate broker. As a potential buyer, you might find a property that looks like a great deal but has millions of dollars of hidden damage, and you can't expect your broker to tell you the ugly truth. I'm not saying not to work with a broker. They provide many useful services, which I'll explain in Chapter 8, but research is not one of their top skills.

Understand that brokers get paid to highlight the positive attributes of a building and facilitate the sale. I like to think of them—as well as anyone else who's financially motivated to make a sale happen—as guilty until proven innocent. Commercial brokers are notorious for delivering pro formas (financial projections provided ahead of a sale) that say, "This property will make you lots of money."

Pro formas often include recommendations along the lines of "spend approximately $250,000 to make some repairs, add new paint, and replace the carpet, and you'll be able to resell this building for $30 per square foot." The problem is that these predictions often end up wildly inaccurate. In my experience, most of the time they're *completely* off and will show you a different world than the one based in reality. The cost of repairs alone may be off by hundreds of thousands of dollars or more, depending on the size of the building— potentially enough to wipe out all expected profits.

I don't believe most brokers act maliciously. Rather, they get their data from the seller, who may be feeding the broker biased or incorrect information. Higher-caliber brokers will usually give more accurate representations of potential values, but even in those cases, the broker won't have performed as thorough an investigation as you'll want to do. I like to follow the principle of "trust but verify" when it comes to brokers and especially the projected pro forma. Rely on your own due diligence to uncover the true cost of repairs and renovations, and you're less likely to be unpleasantly surprised.

You'll have many resources available that you can use to learn more about a property, including:

- County recorder's office: This office will have details about property titles.
- Inspection report: The report will identify problems such as structural issues, water damage, plumbing or electrical problems, pest infestation, and more.
- Legal review: A legal review can uncover liens on the property, contracts, and other issues that might impede the purchasing process.
- Talk to tenants: You don't have to disclose that you are looking at buying the building. After all, maybe you are considering renting there. Ask them if there are any issues, how their experience has been with the property manager, and other questions. I have found issues such as an elevator that worked only half the time and caused tenants to walk up eight flights of stairs simply by talking to the tenants. Do you think that might affect the monthly rent?

- Investment team: You should build a team of real estate experts (which we'll cover in Chapter 8) who can help you evaluate different aspects of a property.

You may not need to tap into each of these resources before deciding *against* a deal, but you'll likely want to utilize all of them and get as deep an understanding as possible before buying a property.

PROPERTY DEAL BREAKERS

Problems with a property in and of themselves aren't deal breakers. In fact, problems should be expected with distressed real estate and are part of the reason you can get such outstanding prices in the first place. A problem only becomes a *problem* when it's financially unfeasible to fix.

TITLE

One of the most significant issues that could be a potential deal breaker is with the title of the property.

> **Title:** In property law, a title is a bundle of rights in a piece of property in which a party may own either a legal interest or equitable interest. The rights in the bundle may be separated and held by different parties. It may also refer to a formal document, such as a deed, that serves as evidence of ownership.

CASE STUDY: WHEN A SELLER COOKS THE BOOKS

Generally, you don't want to trust the information a seller gives you without verifying it first. Let me tell you about a potential apartment building purchase that looked great on paper. The seller claimed the property had a high level of rent collection, but in the due diligence, there was something noticeably strange about the rent collections.

With Class B and C apartment buildings, which tend to have lower-income tenants, money orders and cash payments aren't uncommon, but this property had a suspiciously high percentage of payments from money orders. After a deeper dive into those deposits and requesting copies of the deposits, it was found that most of the money orders came from the same Western Union location not very close to the property.

At this point, it was time for some boots-on-the-ground investigation. It pays to talk directly to tenants because they will give you the information you can't dig up any other way. After knocking on doors and talking to tenants, some tenants apologized for being late on the rent. This didn't make much sense because their payments were shown to be current. It turned out that many residents who'd been listed on the seller's spreadsheet as all paid up hadn't actually paid their rent in several months.

It turned out the seller had been paying tenants' rent himself from a Western Union location near his house to make it look like the building had better rent collection than it did: an over 90 percent payment rate instead of the actual sub-70 percent rate. The deception gave the building a higher exit value because the falsified NOI was not the reality. A new buyer would have quickly found out that the rent collections were drastically lower and would have had to start the eviction process on several tenants at once. The seller had set the sale price at $10 million when a $7 million price would have been more appropriate.

Is this example the broker's fault? Not really, as they weren't thinking about how to verify deposits and see if they were being cooked. Likely, it would have taken months or years to correct that sinking ship, if ever. Although that situation occurred in a good market, what if that had been in a bad market and values were declining?

"Trust but verify."

The title represents the legal structure and ownership of the property or the rights to the property. Owners, lienholders, property tax assessors, federal taxes, equipment (solar panels, cell towers, water systems), tenants, and most certainly, lenders have potential claims to the title and, depending on the jurisdiction, certain rights and processes in which to force a foreclosure or "claim rights."

You might assume that title problems don't occur often, but in the chaos of a recession, they do happen. During the subprime meltdown in 2008, many banks failed, and as a result, their customers' mortgages were transferred to other banks. In the midst of this transfer, where thousands of loans existed only on spreadsheets, some mortgages and titles fell through the cracks.

Over the years, I have researched tens of thousands, and maybe even hundreds of thousands, of properties. There are so many crazy things that come up on title reports and can cause a problem; it almost warrants an entire book on them. Suffice to say, this part of the process should involve a professional, but I will highlight a few of the more common issues.

Lien Position

When buying a foreclosure, knowing the lien position in which you are purchasing is very important. If you were to buy a second lien position (second mortgages or lines of credit), you might still be obligated to pay off the senior loan before you could take ownership.

UCC Liens

UCC liens are common when there is equipment related to a property. An owner can finance the purchase of equipment that is attached to the property, and to protect their rights to the equipment, they will file a UCC lien on the title. Items such as solar panels, water softener systems, and charging stations all apply. I even saw one for an above-ground pool. These liens don't typically go away, and giving the equipment back doesn't necessarily eliminate the lien.

Income Tax Liens

Federal and state governments have the ability to lien all the properties belonging to an owner who owes back taxes. There are timing issues related to these, but let's assume that if someone is losing a multimillion-dollar building, they might also be experiencing other areas of their life where they aren't paying their bills.

I'll say this again as it bears repeating: I highly recommend looking into a property's title as the first step in your due diligence checklist. Everything else about the property could look perfect, but if there's a problem with the title, there's not much you can do about it. Fully researching a property before you buy it can total tens, if not hundreds, of thousands of dollars, so don't waste time on pricier, complicated due diligence tasks when you can investigate the title first. At my real estate company, we've even hired someone away from a title company so they can focus primarily on doing title searches for us—it's that important.

DEBT AND TAXES

Another type of problem that can kill a deal is debt, whether it's owed to lenders or to the state via taxes.

When a property owner owes money and can no longer service their debt, a ripple effect tends to occur. The owner stops spending money on building maintenance and improvements, which, over time, leads to more problems that need more maintenance. The property grows antiquated and, perhaps, damaged. Then a recession hits and breaks the camel's back. The property owner decides to sell their building and rid themselves of the whole situation.

If you don't do proper due diligence, you might unknowingly inherit that debt. For example, there might be other liens against the property accruing fees that we didn't mention before (code enforcement or mechanic's liens to name a few). I mentioned it in the section on lien positions, but there could be multiple mortgages taken out on the building, which triggers a sort of hierarchy that can surprise you later.

I've seen a scenario where a property had two loans on it: a first mortgage for $10 million (called the senior loan because it came first) and a second mortgage for $1 million. A problem had occurred where, due to filing delays, the $1 million "second mortgage" had been filed a day before the first. Here's how a chain of title works: it's not the loan with the larger amount that gets to be in the first position but the one recorded first on a date. In this example, that $1 million loan was the senior loan and the $10 million loan was junior or second position. Loans must be paid off in order, so if you were a buyer looking to purchase the $10 million mortgage, you might be surprised to learn that you would have to pay off that $1 million loan first *before* you could claim your full rights on the $10 million loan. Subsequently, if you were to buy that $1 million loan at foreclosure, you could own that whole property and not have to pay off the $10 million loan.

Although those circumstances are rare today, they were much more common when many loans were being processed at once. Title companies will still sometimes catch this mistake and correct it with a new recording.

Unpaid property taxes can also cause problems for new buyers. Debt to the government takes a super-priority over other debt. You can take out a mortgage on a building, but if there are millions of dollars of property taxes attached to the property, you'll have to pay them. The taxes might have penalties or other fees tacked on, and since the government doesn't give you an option to negotiate them down, they're difficult to resolve short of handing over the money. Certain debts, such as unpaid utility bills, typically are accrued to the owner and get wiped off in a transfer of title, but property tax stays with the property.

Even if the property taxes reach absurd amounts that exceed the actual value of the property, if they go unpaid long enough, the government will take ownership. Depending on the sums involved, debt and tax problems could be a definite deal breaker. I have seen properties with hundreds of thousands in back taxes, yet the property itself was not even worth those back taxes. If you were to be given that property for free, you would still lose money.

DAMAGE AND HAZARDS

Damage and environmental or health hazards can be another deal breaker—something too expensive and difficult to resolve. A building could have issues with mold, water leaks, electricity problems, outdated HVAC, structural problems, or any number of other problems that can be time consuming and costly to fix.

Issues such as hazardous construction materials can also be prohibitively expensive to handle. Occasionally, you'll have to pay more to remove a substance such as asbestos than to tear down the building. Removal costs so much because workers must follow rigorous safety protocols ranging from protective gear to the specific way they bag up and dispose of the debris.

Whether something is "too expensive" relates back to the idea of creating your exit strategy first—the condition and value you anticipate for the property when you go to sell it. If you discover that the cost to get the property in shape for your exit strategy is too much, the damage might be a deal breaker. Unless you can get a higher discount to cancel out the increased repair costs, you won't be able to profitably invest in that property.

For example, imagine finding a property that you anticipate being able to sell for $10 million (we'll assume that's the maximum and takes into account any repurposing or value-add actions), and you can buy it right now for $3 million. On paper, buying a property for 30 percent of its value sounds great! But then you dig into the building's condition and discover that it will require $10 million to fix up. Now there's no way that investment could possibly be profitable. Even if someone gave you the building for free, you'd need to invest $10 million just to sell it for $10 million.

ZONING

Zoning issues are another category of problems that can stop a potential deal dead in its tracks. The first city in the United States to enact zoning codes was Euclid, Ohio. The city planners in Euclid envisioned how their area should be laid out and decided on certain rules, such as factories not being placed directly next to homes. This took place in the early 1900s when, understandably, they didn't want smoke pouring out of a smokestack and into a hospital window. After Euclid, zoning codes became prevalent across the entire country, and they vary by geographic area.

The problem with zoning laws today is that although manufacturing in America has diminished in the last one hundred years, urban areas have expanded. Areas once considered the industrial district now land squarely within urban cores—ideally located pieces of property for apartments, restaurants, and other nonindustrial buildings. Yet, in some markets, zoning laws have not been updated to reflect the change. In others, approval processes move extremely slowly. In California, it could take you a decade to rezone an empty piece of land before you're able to build apartments on it. For this reason, you always want to be aware of how you're allowed to use a piece of property.

Also, if a property was zoned for industrial use in the past and is now eligible for other uses, you'll want to check for any kind of contamination. Most people expect properties such as gas stations to have some level of chemical contamination, but in terms of difficulty and cost to clean up, dry cleaners are actually far worse. Certain chemicals can get into the soil and be a nightmare to decontaminate, so be sure to look into the history of a property before assuming contamination won't be an issue.

Contamination is one of the most significant issues in the redevelopment of older industrial properties. Getting a phase 1 and phase 2 environmental inspection can be difficult or impossible to get if the property is going through the foreclosure process. The reason being is they involve drilling into the soil and getting samples. Let's just assume that most owners going through foreclosure won't typically be too keen on the idea of a random stranger showing up with a rig and drilling for soil test samples.

Contamination might not be a deal breaker for you, but it's certainly a challenge. Like each of these other issues, it needs to align with your exit strategy and investment plan for the deal to be viable. Be aware of the realistic costs and factor them into your profit equation.

DUE DILIGENCE CHECKLIST

Brokers aren't going to disclose accurate information about a building's condition—they might not even have it. You need to perform your own investigation and unearth the details so you know what you're getting into with a property.

Whereas residential real estate has certain consumer protection laws requiring pages of disclosures before you buy a house, commercial real estate has relatively few. The commercial side of the industry doesn't hold your hand, so it's important to go into the process informed and with a plan. You may have only a limited amount of time to access a property before you need to make a purchasing decision.

As you're inspecting a property, here are just a few of the questions you'll want to be answered:

- Are there any problems with the property's title?
- Are there any liens against the property? Any debt? Unpaid property taxes?
- Is the building up to code? If not, what needs to change? Do you need to resolve code violations before renting out the property?

- If it's an older building, were any hazardous building materials used in its construction, such as lead paint, toxic glue for vinyl tiles, asbestos, or other toxic or carcinogenic substances?
- If you're changing the use of a property—for example, turning an industrial building into apartment lofts—are there any zoning problems? What about chemical contamination?

The questions above should be asked about every property you consider, regardless of its use or niche.

WORK WITHIN YOUR PLAN

At its core, due diligence is the process of identifying any of the problems listed above and determining whether they're too significant to be able to execute your business plan. The presence of one or more of these problems in a property, while a red flag, isn't an automatic disqualification. You may be able to adjust your plan, secure a steeper discount, counterbalance the cost in some way, or otherwise make the deal work. The important thing is that any obstacles fit within your plan and that the deal makes financial sense at the end of the day.

Treat each red flag that pops up as an opportunity to check in with your plan. Ask, "If this turns out to be an issue, will my exit strategy still work?"

CASE STUDY: TOO EXPENSIVE TO FIX

Years ago, I considered bidding on the Ingalls Building, a historic building in downtown Cincinnati, Ohio. At that time, it sat vacant despite being a beautiful building and on the historic landmark registry as the first reinforced concrete skyscraper in the world. It was also being sold for what appeared to be an excellent price on paper: $3 million.

During my due diligence, I learned that because the building had gone vacant, it triggered the need for a new certificate of occupancy. Certain codes had been grandfathered in for as long as the building remained occupied, but when economic distress caused people to move out, the grandfather clause ended. That meant the next owner would have to do a remodel to bring anything that had fallen out of compliance up to code.

The biggest problem was that the building had only one staircase or fire escape route. To bring the property up to code, the new owners would need to add a second staircase, which would require cutting away a large part of each of its seventeen floors. Alternatively, one of the solutions I tried to put together was to purchase the building next to it (which was not for sale at the time) and add an external staircase. But given the timing of the auction and the inability to get control over that next-door property in a timely matter, it posed a significant issue.

With this new information, the cost to fix up the building had risen far beyond the expected cosmetics and modernization of new-windows, mechanicals-and-paint remodel. It required a major structural modification to even qualify for a certificate of occupancy. The price no longer fit into my investment strategy or exit plan, so I did not bid on the property. Had I not uncovered the staircase requirement and bought the property, I would have lost money on the deal. By the way, since the elevator was out of service, hiking up and down seventeen flights of stairs several times to do due diligence was a great way to drive home the need for due diligence.

You don't have to go through the entire due diligence process before turning down a deal. For example, you might discover that a property used to house a dry-cleaning business. Checking for contamination is not an easy or cheap process. You need someone to collect soil samples and send them off to be analyzed, but if the property is going through foreclosure, you might not have permission to show up and start digging. At this point, you could reasonably decide that between the missing information and the costs to move forward with the due diligence process, it isn't worth it for you to continue with the deal. Backing out is okay and even necessary. Not every deal will be a winner. It's better to stick to your risk tolerance now than overlook a problem and pay for it later.

As another word of warning, you'll want to make sure to stay objective throughout the due diligence process. It's not unusual for investors, especially new investors, to get emotionally invested in a property. Imagine, you've identified a beautiful, historic building for sale. You've looked at it and told your spouse about it. You've walked through its floors and envisioned how you might elevate its use. Now red flags start to pop up, and because you're emotionally invested in this property, you want to overlook them. But that's a poor way of doing business, and if you ignore a red flag that turns out to be a major problem, you'll set yourself up for significant failure.

Nobody will step in and save you from a bad deal. As I

mentioned before, commercial real estate has far fewer consumer protections than residential real estate. If you miss or overlook red flags and buy a property that ends up having serious problems, you technically have a path to legal recourse, but it will be a battle. There's a good chance that even if you lose millions of dollars on the deal, your bank will tell you, "Good luck. You're on your own."

I've also witnessed someone buy a property after not doing their due diligence, only to realize they'd made a mistake shortly after the foreclosure auction ended. They actually tried to cancel the cashier's check they'd used to buy the property, even going so far as to make an official statement claiming the check had been stolen. Of course it hadn't. The buyer had simply made a poor decision, and all they managed to do was make a bad situation worse. That day, they learned the importance of doing your due diligence before buying—and that the FBI takes bank fraud very seriously.

Here's another likely scenario: You attend a foreclosure auction. Other investors are there, and they have done more thorough due diligence than you. They know a piece of property has serious issues. They see you bidding on that property, and they *know* you'll lose money on it. But guess what? They aren't going to say anything. They won't warn, stop, or protect you from the huge mistake you're about to make. If you buy that property and lose money, it only means less competition for them going forward. That's the reality of this business: you need to watch out for yourself.

Thoroughly researching a property and objectively weighing any red flags against your investment plan is the only way to minimize your risk and set yourself up for success. Maybe it would be exciting to own that beautiful old building, but as an investment property, it's a business. It's dollars and cents on a balance sheet, and if those numbers don't add up in your favor, you absolutely should not do the deal.

TIPS AND TAKEAWAYS: DON'T BUY THIS PROPERTY

- Some properties have such costly or time-consuming problems that they aren't worth considering, even if someone gave you the building for free.
- To avoid accidentally buying an unviable property, you have to do your due diligence. Nobody else will warn you about the true cost of fixing up or rehab a property.
- Investigate the property and learn why the current owners are selling it or why it's going into foreclosure; what's causing the distress; how much the property will cost to fix; and whether the income potential for the building has changed.
- Don't trust the pro forma your real estate broker gives you. These financial projections tend to be wildly inaccurate.

- Problems that can constitute deal breakers include title issues, debt, unpaid taxes, damage, contamination or other hazards, and zoning issues.
- Follow a due diligence checklist to ensure that you don't miss any potentially costly problems.
- Major problems with a property are only deal breakers if they don't align with your exit strategy. If you can resolve the issues and still make a profit, the deal may still be viable.

CHAPTER EIGHT

TEAMWORK MAKES THE DREAM WORK: CREATING YOUR INVESTMENT TEAM

Even if you're on the right track, you'll get run over if you just sit there.

—WILL ROGERS

Throughout this book, I've given you an overview of the commercial real estate investing world. However, no single person can master every aspect of this business. In fact, you can spend a lifetime in a single category of the real estate business and still learn something new every day.

I would know. I've worked in real estate for over twenty

years now. I have worked as a general contractor, I have a master's degree in real estate, a broker's license, and I've completed the courses as a Certified Commercial Investment Member (CCIM) candidate. But I'm not an expert in everything—nobody is—and that's why I have team members whose skillsets complement my own.

It takes a group to conquer the different challenges you'll encounter as you work to make financial freedom a reality, so let's start building your team.

KEY ROLES ON YOUR INVESTMENT TEAM

Real estate is a team sport, which is why this chapter focuses on building out your roster of professionals: who should be on your team and why you need them. Especially when you're first starting out, you'll want to take advantage of other people's knowledge and specialties. They'll fill in the gaps in your own knowledge base and help you stack the deck in your favor. As motivational speaker Jim Rohn famously said, "You are the average of the five people you spend the most time with." Surround yourself with successful real estate professionals, and there's a good chance they'll rub off on you.

There are a handful of core roles you'll want on your team, regardless of your market or asset class: investor, operator, contractor, broker, lender, inspectors, and attorneys.

Let's go through each of them and explore the parts they play in the overall investment process.

INVESTOR, MONEY, OR EQUITY

All of these titles are synonymous with who is putting in the money. This can be you, a single investor (maybe a rich uncle), a group of people in the deal together, or it can be something like syndication or a fund. With commercial real estate, having this figured out before you start buying properties is going to be paramount to your success. We talked about this earlier: As a new investor, you might not need investors or capital if you are "wholesaling" a deal, but you will need to know who has the money to buy it from you. Also, note that if you are buying the property and using financing, lenders will often want to see a personal net worth from the ownership group that is equal to or greater than the asset you are buying. You may need someone to be able to sign on a loan with you if you don't personally have the net worth. This is an easier ask if the loan is "nonrecourse" than the much more significant ask if limited or full recourse. If you find a great deal but have no one to wholesale it to or to invest into it, then it doesn't matter how potentially good the deal might be.

OPERATOR OR SPONSOR

Who is going to manage this investment? Who is going to

pay the bills, organize the architects and lenders, and coordinate everything? This role might be fulfilled by one of the people on your team, it might be a combined effort, or it might be a firm that you invest with. In any arrangement, it is incredibly important to know who is going to coordinate all the items. If your investment strategy is to buy land and sit and wait, then this likely isn't much more than an accountant or bookkeeper. If the goal is to repurpose an office to an apartment, then this role will likely require a highly specialized and experienced person. Your investment criteria will determine who that might need to be.

Also, note that these other roles assume that you are buying an existing building and there is some level of distress that needs to be addressed, ranging from light cosmetic physical distress to significant redevelopment.

CONTRACTOR

A contractor is one of the most important people you'll want on your investment team. If you remember my story from the book's Introduction about getting started in real estate, there's a reason the successful real estate developer at the country club gave twenty-three-year-old me this piece of advice: Become a contractor.

As a trades role in the thick of the construction process, contractors have a deep understanding of how the physical side of real estate works. They know how properties get built, how to move dirt or build roads, how to remodel a building, and how much time each construction activity will take. Granted, not every contractor specializes in each of those areas, but most should understand the sequence of events that needs to happen to fix up a distressed property.

A contractor will be able to quickly assess the condition of a property and will likely notice problems that other people miss. For example, they might notice faint, barely visible cracks in the brick and mortar that indicate a more serious structural problem. Recall from the last chapter that finding these red flags during your due diligence process is key to accurately calculate your profit margin. If you don't know the true cost of repairs before you buy, you can't possibly plan your exit strategy from the start.

In addition to identifying problems with the property, a contractor will help you estimate the cost to execute your exit plan. Let's say that you want to raise the value of a property you own to $10 million. You know the building needs work, but you're not sure how much it will cost to get it to that value. A contractor will assess the property, determine what needs to happen, and estimate how much it will cost. They might tell you, "The building needs $4 million worth of work." The more detailed an estimate they can make, the better because you can then factor that cost into your ROI equation.

Every other person on this list will provide more transactional interactions, but ideally, you'll develop a deeper, ongoing relationship with your contractor or contractors. As I mentioned earlier in the book, a contractor can even be the perfect partner. The more you work together, the more your contractor will understand your investment strategy and the costs you need to manage. Furthermore, contractors typically have a built-in profit margin, but if you bring your contractor into the deal and give them equity in the property, they'll likely charge less for the work they provide. In this way, you can potentially save a ton on contracting costs.

Until you have a partner contractor or a go-to contractor that you trust, make sure to get multiple contractor bids for every project. There's a huge amount of variation in potential pricing between companies. A large construction firm with 150 employees and a ton of overhead might charge much more than a small ten-person company with no office. Cheaper isn't always better—after all, they need to be able to do the work—but by shopping around and knowing your options, you can possibly save hundreds of thousands of dollars or more.

REAL ESTATE BROKER

The second person you want on your investment team is a real estate broker. The broker will manage several jobs, including finding properties, sourcing deals, and delivering market data.

You'll want to find a broker who specializes in your target market and asset class, whether that's the retail market, industrial properties, or other commercial real estate assets. They'll be the person most likely to find you deals that fit your investment profile so you can act quickly and beat the competition. A great broker will compile detailed information that helps you in your due diligence. For example, if you invest in office buildings, they might generate a list of every office building in your market's downtown area, including when tenants' leases renew and how much they're paying per square foot. They'll help you entice tenants to rent *your* buildings instead of your competitors' as you gradually grow your portfolio.

Keep in mind that brokers are usually working with incomplete information. As I explained in the previous chapter, the data they receive from sellers might be incorrect, and they aren't doing as deep an investigation into properties as you need. Their pro forma, the financial projection for a property, tends to be far more optimistic than reality.

In short, brokers aren't perfect. They work on commission, so they have an inherent incentive to make sales happen, and that may add bias to their advice. But despite these drawbacks, they still provide information valuable to your exit strategy and plan. They can also become valuable partners. I have included brokers in a deal if they were able to find me the deals, bring a key tenant, or create value, such as creative financing because of their relationship with the owner. Good brokers tend to have their finger on the pulse of the market and can provide quick judgment calls, which is especially helpful when you first consider a deal and want a high-level overview of a property's potential. As a member of your team who knows the local network, they can also identify which other brokers tend to paint a rosier pro forma than even the normal margin of error. They'll act as an analyst for your deals overall, and they'll do much of the legwork in finding properties that fit your investment strategy.

LENDER OR CAPITAL MARKETS

Your next team member is your lender or capital markets group. As I covered in Chapter 6, you have many different options for financing: traditional lenders (banks or debt funds), cash, negotiation, retirement funds, seller financing, master lease, alternative lenders (hard money or private lenders), and partnerships. Some of these options require partnering, or at least working closely, with the people supplying your funds.

Naturally, a lending partner has the most potential to become a long-term member of your investment team.

CASE STUDY: MARGIN CALLED

I was working on a $25 million deal and had a fully approved loan for $18.5 million. We were set to close on a Monday after months of negotiations and back-and-forth with inspectors, lawyers, and the full gambit of people involved in a purchase. We had a full set of loan docs and were signing them on Friday. The seller even alerted all the tenants that we would be taking over the building on Monday. We were signing a conference room table's worth of paperwork, when early in the morning, we noticed some typos on some signature pages.

The lender's legal team sent over corrected documents, but later in the afternoon, we noticed another typo. This time, something strange happened. I am not sure if you've ever experienced this, but we sent emails and had this eerie feeling. Something wasn't right. The lender's attorney stopped responding. Right away, this compounded the feeling, so after a few missed calls, we had our capital markets group call, too. Finally, our capital markets person got through to one of his insider folks, and we found out that the lender had been getting margin called all week, and they no longer had the funds to close the loan. This happened on Friday, and we were supposed to close in three days on Monday!

Suddenly, we found ourselves in a nightmare situation where I was hard on the $1 million down (meaning if this deal didn't close, I would lose a million dollars), but now, just before closing, I was being told our lender didn't have the funds to close the deal. I'm sure there were other investment groups that had the capabilities to handle this, but I was standing flat-footed and had no way to come up with the money for closing in three days. We had done everything that we could do—we estimated the work using contractors, appraised the value of the property, considered our broker's market analysis, double- and triple-checked the numbers—but because our lender had been margin called and had their future funding lines frozen, I was staring down the barrel of losing $1 million.

Let's just say going home on what should have been a celebrated weekend turned into going home and telling my wife I might lose $1 million, which could have put us in a significantly dangerous financial position. Thank the Lord! My wife is such an amazing woman; she said, "Well, okay, do what you can do." It was still an anxious weekend, but it sure helps to have a supportive spouse.

Fortunately, I had developed a good relationship with the seller over the purchase process and was able to negotiate some extra time for closing. We were able to bring in another lender and close the deal, but we almost lost out. Had I not had the help of that capital markets group (Ken Karmolinski—Divergent Capital), I likely would have lost $1 million on that deal.

Your project may need a purchase money loan, a construction loan, and then need to refinance into a permanent loan all within a short period of your exit plan. I have found that working with a capital markets group can be significantly beneficial. They can be a source for both debt and equity on good deals. They also know many of their lenders personally, as this has been their career for decades. Nothing is worse than a lender that gives you a term sheet, and then pulls their offer at the last minute or tries to retrade you on terms. A good capital markets broker will be able to help you vet someone, determine whether they can close or not, and determine the pros and cons of them as a lender.

Your bank might serve as a sort of team member, but

remember, during recessions, banks and other traditional lenders tend to stop or cut back on lending. They might offer a 70 percent loan-to-value (LTV) ratio before, but as soon as a recession starts, they reduce it to 60 percent. Maybe they previously lent at 5 percent interest; now they lend at 10 percent. Not only do lenders not *want* to finance purchases during recessions, but they may not even be able to.

As my "Margin Called" case study illustrates, there are two lessons to learn here. First, this is a relationship business, and had I tried to get every last dollar out of the seller up front or had a strained relationship with them, I am not sure they would have given us the extra time. Second, you want to have a good team to help pick you up when the unexpected happens. Even if you do your due diligence— we had paid the lender tens of thousands of dollars to prevent things like this from happening—problems occur, so it pays to know your team. Ensure that you're asking the right questions of your lender and that they have a plan in place to solve problems that might come up in a recession. You're relying on them to make your deal possible, so if they don't have answers to your concerns, find someone new.

INSPECTORS

The fourth member of your team is the inspector, or some-times, a contracted boots-on-the-ground person. Several potential people can perform the role of the inspector, including an inspector, engineer, or architect, depending on the project's needs. Many commercial buildings have complex systems, so if you're looking at an office building or hotel, for example, you might need someone who specializes in heating and air conditioning.

Generally, the inspector checks for code compliance and the condition of the building and its systems. Remember my story about the Ingalls Building in Cincinnati from the previous chapter? The inspector brought up the fact that because it was out of service, it was no longer grandfathered in and that the building needed a second staircase. They gave me the information I needed to make an informed buying decision about that building, and an inspector will do the same for you.

The inspector will also play a critical role in repurposing a building. Imagine wanting to convert an asset that's failing as an office building into apartments. To know whether it's a viable project, you need to determine if the utility infrastructure can handle apartments. Will there be enough electricity, water, and drainage capacity?

The person in your inspector role—likely an engineer in this example—can inspect the property and determine whether you need to upgrade the plumbing system, electrical wiring, or other feature. These upgrades can easily cost hundreds of thousands or millions of dollars to implement in an entire building, so you'll want an experienced specialist to give their opinion. You never want to assume the water, electrical, and other systems work fine in a building without confirming with an inspection.

Not only can these systems cause enormously expensive problems if they aren't maintained or upgraded properly, but even worse, they present serious safety hazards. Older buildings, in particular, tend to have undersized wiring for modern uses, which can overheat and catch fire. Don't take that risk with your properties or people's lives: hire an inspector who specializes in the areas you need.

ATTORNEY

Last, you'll want to have skilled attorneys on your team to handle any legal matters. Attorneys are like doctors and tend to specialize in certain areas of the law. A securities attorney might be great at setting up your legal entities but be way out of their league on zoning and land use laws. Understanding many facets of your plan will help you better determine the attorneys you will need to work with. Some questions that will be helpful to ask are things such as: How are you going to buy the property? Where are you going to raise money? Are you going to buy the property by yourself or with a partner or group? Are you going to set this up as a fund?

When financing a purchase, especially if you're raising

money from other people, you can quickly run into certain security laws that can get you in trouble. For example, if you contact ten of your friends and say, "I want you to invest in this building with me," and they each give you a few hundred thousand dollars, suddenly you have a private security offering, which must follow regulations from the federal government. Your attorney can ensure that any funds follow the proper structure. They'll follow proper legal codes, file the paperwork, and generally prevent you from unpleasant legal struggles as you set up the purchase. Further into the purchasing process, an attorney will also review lease agreements, loan documents, and other contracts.

Throughout the investing process, you can expect to sign hundreds and thousands of pages of documents. Especially in the beginning, will you feel confident that you understand what you're signing? Are you *sure* you aren't agreeing to hand over your firstborn if you miss a mortgage payment?

Your attorney's job is to make sure you understand exactly what you agree to: the risks, commitments, and consequences. You can bet that lenders give their contracts teeth. They want to make sure that they benefit from the arrangement, and if you don't know their expectations, you can end up paying a lot in unexpected fees. However, you should know that one of the benefits of commercial real estate is that you can negotiate everything, including your loan documents and contracts. You are not afforded that same luxury in residential loans. If you don't like the way the loan documents are structured, tough luck. But if you remember from earlier, there are many consumer laws that pertain to residential property purchase versus commercial real estate. If a lender words something too ambiguously in the loan terms, your attorney can argue to change it. If you don't like the terms for any reason, you don't necessarily have to agree to them.

Your attorney is unequivocally on your side, so if they do their job well, you can feel confident that you're as legally protected as possible.

FINDING YOUR TEAM MEMBERS

Now that you know the five core roles on your investment team, you can start finding eligible candidates right away. You don't need to—and shouldn't—wait until you've bought your first property before making connections. Start now. Create a list of people who have the specialties and skill-sets you'll need for future investments. If you get a jump on networking, you'll have your contacts ready to go when your opportunity to catch a falling knife arrives.

Referrals can be a great way to learn about experienced professionals with the talents you need, so try asking other real estate investors in your market for names. You can also search for potential candidates online; just be sure to vet them thoroughly. Ask about experience, skillsets, policies, and insist on speaking to references.

Remember, it is not always about an impressive résumé but having the specific talents and knowledge that *your* investment projects require.

TIPS AND TAKEAWAYS: CREATING YOUR INVESTMENT TEAM

- No single person can be an expert in all things real estate, so you'll want to have a team of professionals to complement your investing skillset.
- Your core investing team should include the following five roles: contractor, broker, lender, inspector, and attorney.
- You'll likely need other, more-specialized roles depending on the specific nature of your project. For example, you might need an interior designer for a hotel or a contamination specialist for an industrial site.
- Start assembling your team now, before you buy your first property. Aim to have your network established before the next recession so you'll be ready to seize promising opportunities.

CHAPTER NINE

STRATEGIES FOR FINDING THE BEST DEALS

The safest and most potentially profitable thing is to buy something when no one likes it.

—HOWARD MARKS

Foreclosures offer the steepest discounts and most exciting opportunities for commercial real estate investors, but what if you want more deals?

Perhaps there aren't many foreclosures in your market, or you simply want to consider every opportunity available to you. Fortunately, you have options.

Finding these properties might take a bit more work than

identifying foreclosures, but if you can contact the owner or bank *before* the loan even falls into default, you can potentially work out a deal without any competition whatsoever.

THE STAGES OF DISTRESS

A property doesn't have to go fully into foreclosure to be impacted by distress. Different stages of distress put different pressures on properties and their owners, and by understanding them, you'll know the signals of a good deal in the making. There are typically three stages to distressed properties: public market distress, private market distress, and deep distress.

If you know what to look for in each of these stages, you can be poised to act at exactly the right moment—when the property owner wants to sell but hasn't yet defaulted on their mortgage.

PUBLIC MARKET DISTRESS

The first signs of distress, the hint of an impending recession, tend to start in the public market. When this begins, you see real estate investment trusts (REITs) and stock valuations slow down or start to decline. As soon as the market slows down, lenders quickly halt lending, too.

During this stage, you can expect margin calls to happen

behind the scenes (*remember what happened to my margin-called lender? This is exactly what happened*), which can trigger opportunities for deals that can't get financing. For example, in the 2008 subprime meltdown, investment firms such as Bear Stearns and Lehman Brothers began getting margin calls when their accounts ran out of money, and they went bankrupt. It all began with subdued, but not necessarily secret, turmoil in the public market.

If you notice this turmoil before it escalates, you can prepare to act quickly when distress drives discounts in property prices.

PRIVATE MARKET DISTRESS

Once the market distress worsens, it will start affecting the private markets. Property owners and institutional investors will begin taking proactive steps to limit their losses by pruning their portfolios. They can see capital calls and other potential problems coming down the pipeline and adjust their behavior accordingly. They're trying to avoid foreclosure, even if it means losing some underperforming properties now. (See "Case Study: Hotel Nightmare or Dream?" in Chapter 5.)

How the private market reacts will, of course, depend on the nature of the recession. Which assets are impacted—houses, hospitality, office buildings? You want to understand how the recession is starting so you can also predict its trajectory. For example, the COVID-19 pandemic locked down the hospitality industry, which caused ripple effects in surrounding businesses. If a convention center closed, the restaurants and shops around it lost business, too, even if they remained open.

Many businesses file for bankruptcy during this stage, which means an incoming flood of properties coming onto the market.

DEEP DISTRESS

Last, we have the third stage, deep distress. With deep distress, something has happened to significantly change the market. Tenant demand may have decreased, a major company or industry could have moved out of an area (like what transpired in Detroit), a pandemic shut down the economy, or some other event occurred that triggered a deeper recession.

In this stage, properties start going through the foreclosure process, which means as a commercial real estate investor, you can find the most deeply discounted deals. However, as I said, you don't have to wait until deep distress to find great deals. As investors prune their portfolios, you can buy discounted properties in the earlier stages, too.

FINDING DEALS

Earlier in the book, I discussed how you could search public notices to find foreclosures in your market, but there could also be properties *not* going into foreclosure that present excellent buying opportunities. Imagine a property owner who hasn't defaulted on their loan yet but is barely scraping by. They might be happy to rid themselves of the property and sell it to you for a discount.

If there aren't public notices for these properties, how can you find them?

As you'll see, a combination of tapping into your network, visual searching, and outreach can unearth some exceptional secret deals.

USE YOUR NETWORK

As far as valuable life skills go, networking ranks toward the top, regardless of what you do for a living. Real estate is no exception. Starting immediately, you'll want to build a network of knowledgeable people in the real estate space: real estate brokers, lenders, contractors, investor clubs and groups, and anyone else who might have insight into properties in your market.

When you search for nonforeclosure deals, your network is the first place to start. As you get to know people in these spheres, communicate to them what you're looking for in a property. The more specific you can define what you are looking for, the more likely you are to have someone find it. But build relationships, and as people learn about the type of deals you're looking for, they'll be more likely to tell you about off-market opportunities that fit your criteria. For example, people in your network might know if a local property owner is falling behind on payments or if another investor may be getting margin calls. If they want to help, they'll either tell the other person, "I know an investor who might take this property off your hands," or they'll approach you about contacting the person going through distress. Either way, your connections can help put you in touch with people who might sell you a property at a great discount.

Be aware, however, that as someone new to this space, it will take some time to build out your network and create connections. People in the business tend to have a small circle of investors they contact first with new deals, often before the properties ever make it on the market publicly. You won't be in the inner circle of brokers and lenders in your market from day one, but you can get there. Fortunately, a recession should help you speed up those connections, or at least get insider information more readily. Brokers tend to be much hungrier for a commission and, therefore, more forthcoming with information during times of market distress. If you include people in this network as partners, this is also a great way to speed up being in the inner circle. *(Be careful, as this can be a double-edged sword. If you give someone too much of a deal or improperly structure it, the mistake can be very costly to correct. Trust me, I have done this poorly in the past and it cost me a lot of money.)*

To jump-start your professional network, browse Facebook groups, meetup.com, and other websites to find an investor group in your area. This can be a great way to meet the active players in your market as well as hear the local property gossip. You'll likely be surprised to hear how quickly news about distressed properties spreads in these circles.

Can You Trust Your Network?

At this point, you might be saying, "Hold on, Jake. Earlier in the book, you said investors at an auction would watch silently as I threw my life savings away. Can I actually trust my network?"

Here's the thing: There's a big difference between competing with others for a specific property *right now* and networking with people who happen to operate in the same city. There's a good chance you aren't even directly competing with the other people in your real estate networking club. You might focus on different asset classes, risk tolerances, or budgets. Brokers and lenders, unless they're also investors, won't be competing with you at all. You'll all benefit from sharing information and working together, not suffer for it.

Granted, you shouldn't expect to hear minute details about the deals people *are* pursuing. They'll hold those specifics close to their chests. But most of the time, your contacts will know about opportunities they aren't personally interested in, and they'll be happy to share. Especially when you're new, many more-experienced investors will gladly throw down the rope and help pull you up rather than try to keep you down.

I have had fierce battles over properties and bidding wars with competitors, only to then go and have drinks later. Many times, my competitors have become partners on future deals.

If you have doubts about a person's motivations and suspect they might be acting in bad faith, trust your gut. I've always believed that humans have a good innate sense of whether something's off. Also, ask yourself, *If I were in their position, would I give me this advice? Would I share the details about this deal?*

If there's something suspicious about what they're telling you, walk away. Most people you meet will want to succeed together, but you might encounter people who would take advantage of you, too. Your best defense is always to listen to your instincts.

VISUALLY IDENTIFY DISTRESSED PROPERTIES

Another option to uncover secret deals is to keep an eye out for visually distressed properties. Drive, walk, or my new favorite way, scooter around your market and look for boarded-up real estate, buildings with signs of deferred maintenance, and dilapidated structures. These are all clues that the property owner has struggled to keep up with payments and the cost to maintain their building.

There's no guarantee that the property owner will be open to selling, but in my experience, a neglected building is a good indication that they're going through distress.

DIRECTLY CONTACT OWNERS

Another option, which I discussed earlier in the book, will work in this context, too: directly contacting property owners. Run a direct mail campaign in your market asking property owners to reach out to you if they want to sell.

Technology makes collecting the contact information for business owners in your market easy. I prefer using an app called Land Glide, which allows you to quickly pull up tax records for properties. Make a list of mailing addresses for properties that owe taxes, send out your letter, and wait for the bites to roll in. Some people love using "bandit signs" with your contact details and a short description of the asset type you're looking to buy. There's a good chance that an exhausted property owner or two will be ready to wash their hands of their building. I personally have not played much in the wholesaling space and have found it better to locate a good wholesaler and share what you are looking for, as they will hustle and find the deals for you.

FIND GOOD DEALS, CREATE GREAT ONES

To be truly successful in real estate, you need to be proactive, not passive. Adopt an entrepreneurial hunger and go after the best deals you can make. Rarely are those the ones listed in the public forum that everyone can access; they'll be the deals you hunted down and negotiated yourself.

I spend countless hours researching tax records and finding out who owns what properties. I'm then able to map out who the players are in each market. If you remember from earlier, as part of my due diligence team, I have a title research expert. We will cross-reference mailing addresses and signature pages on documents to find out where people live. We'll pull up personal mortgages, skip trace them, and look for social media accounts, all to see if there is something that we can discover that might help us in finding a deal or something that might make a compelling offer. Call it being a real estate stalker.

This also helps me find the outliers. For example, when I am looking at investing in a new market, I do a *deep* dive into property records. One time, one of the properties I found was in downtown San Antonio. It was an office building owned by an oil and gas company in Fort Worth. I then wondered why they owned that building. When I dug deeper, I learned that it was the only property they owned in the whole city, and they had owned it for ten to fifteen years. Also, they took title to it in a fund. *Hmm, that's interesting,* I thought. That gave me several nuggets of information. Being an out-of-town owner that bought with a fund more than ten years ago meant they'd likely be willing to sell the property if the offer was appropriate. It looked like the building wasn't critical to their operations, as the main office building might have been. Building on that information, I did a significant amount of research on that property long before it ever came on the market.

Keep in mind that your competition has the same widely available information as you, so to get ahead of them, you need to dig up data they haven't found. Scour your market, connect with owners, understand why their property is in distress, and then offer them a way out.

TIPS AND TAKEAWAYS: STRATEGIES FOR FINDING THE BEST DEALS

- Foreclosures create opportunities to buy at a discount, but if you can identify distress before the foreclosure process even starts, you can find equally great deals with less competition.

- Understand what's happening with properties during the three stages of distress: public market distress, private market distress, and deep distress.
- Use different strategies to identify potential deals in your market: networking and professional contacts, visual signs of property distress, and direct contact with owners using mailers or flyers.
- You'll find the best deals not through the same shared resources your competitors are using but by proactively searching for distressed properties and willing sellers.

CONCLUSION

*Courage taught me no matter how bad a crisis gets...any sound
investment will eventually pay off.*

—CARLOS SLIM HELU

In the twenty-plus years I've worked in commercial real
estate investing, the best deals I've done happened in times
of recession or distress. These periods, without a doubt,
create the most opportunity to buy property at prices that
are disjointed from usual market values. Not only will you
find more deals during these times, but also those deals
will be more forgiving to you as a beginner. They'll have a
higher profit margin and more room for error as you take
the advice in this book and put it into practice.

Best of all, if you follow the strategies I've shown you for
finding, evaluating, and financing deals, you'll be able to

reach out and catch falling knives without cutting yourself. These once-in-a-decade deals can put you on the path to financial freedom and even generational wealth. I'm not saying this is an easy path. It's not a get-rich-quick scheme, and you will experience times of stress and doubt. But with hard work, you can and will create success.

As I work through this book, there are so many more ideas or concepts I would love to go over. But I remind myself that this is not a textbook, and my hope is that this is a starting point for you to dig deeper, like the book *Rich Dad, Poor Dad* was for me. It was a starting point. So my goal with this book has been to provide you with an organized, linear, high-level look into the world of commercial real estate investing. It's a starting point from which you can dive deeper and focus your interests. Furthermore, it's a guide that can give you direction as you explore the firehose of free information available on the internet.

Hopefully, by this point, you've started thinking about the market and asset class you'd like to work within. What type of property excites you? What will hold your interest for years to come? What will define your investment strategy?

Maybe you'll choose to buy hotels with financing from an alternative lender and convert them to apartments, or purchase apartment buildings that generate passive income with your contractor partner, or sign master leases on restaurants in secondary cities for your ghost kitchen empire. Part of what makes commercial real estate so exciting is that you can find exactly the investment strategy that's best for you. You choose the time frame, risk, location, effort—everything. Success is all about taking the investment path that will help you achieve financial freedom in a way that fits your goals. An appropriate and good investment for you might be a terrible investment for me because our skillsets, experiences, and interests differ.

Your strategy is exactly that: *your* strategy.

I would never recommend investing in an asset that you dislike just because you think it's what you're supposed to do. The reality is that commercial real estate is a wide and varied industry with room to pursue the locations, investments, and asset classes that interest you. Remember, whether a deal is "good" comes down to one simple question: When all of the different variables add up—the property value minus the cost of purchasing, the cost of fixing the property, and transactional costs—do you make a profit worth the amount of time, money, and effort you put into the deal?

If the answer is yes, it means the deal fits your investment strategy, and you should do it. Choose the niche that appeals to you the most and learn all that you can.

TAKE THE NEXT STEP TOWARD FINANCIAL FREEDOM

Now that you've reached the end of this book, the parting message I want to leave you with is this: Go forward and take action. Like reading about push-ups, this book won't help you improve your life unless you put the information to work and take the next step.

At the time you're reading this, there may or may not be a recession. It doesn't matter—you can take action right now. Learn more, build your network, and shape your investment plan. The sooner you start, the more prepared you'll be to catch falling knives when the moment strikes.

If you're feeling overwhelmed, you don't have to go down this path alone. In fact, as I described earlier in the book, it's better if you don't. I recommend building a team around yourself and learning from the experience and skillsets of others. Throughout my career, I've learned plenty of valuable lessons from my own mistakes and successes, but I've gained just as many, if not more, from the help and guidance of others. Your team members will help you collect as much information as possible about properties you're considering so you can create exit strategies based on accurate valuations. The more you know going into a purchase, the more confident you'll be in your projected profits.

Now, what happens if you buy a property or two and decide that this path isn't right for you?

The good news is that you don't need to abandon commercial real estate investing entirely. Instead of buying and managing properties yourself, you might choose to invest in a fund or become a private lender. You can balance the time and risk you put into investing with the reward you get out of it. Multiple paths can lead to the financial freedom you desire.

Maybe this book will also cast light on the fact that there are a ton of things to learn that you don't know and perhaps aren't interested in learning about. You might already be making six and seven figures at your day job and you don't have the time or interest in doing the nitty-gritty of this business. There is nothing wrong with that. I have many doctor clients who realize it's better to go to a specialist than try and wing it. An ophthalmologist (eye doctor) who has a foot problem doesn't treat themselves; they go see a podiatrist (foot doctor). Just because they both went and trained as doctors does not make them equal in solving foot problems.

I know many of my clients are smarter than I am, especially in areas that they specialize in. They are uniquely trained and talented in the fields of medicine, engineering, law, or whatever they do. That is because they specialize in one area, and they will be much better at solving problems in that area as a result.

I would encourage you to continue learning no matter

where you are in that process, whether you're just starting out, like myself years ago, or you're already a high-income earner looking to get off the hamster wheel. If this book spurs you to action, it has more than done its job.

LEARN MORE

If distressed commercial real estate investing sounds like the right path for you and you want a deeper dive—after all, I intended for this book to give you a look at the industry and a high-level strategy, not for it to be a textbook—check out many free resources at **catchknives. com** and look for my Distressed Commercial Real Estate Investing MasterClass series. That series allows me to dive much deeper into topics I briefly covered in this book and it provides hours of detailed information on dozens of topics, from creating a pro forma to evaluating properties, so you can build on the foundational knowledge you gained from this book. Or if you are an accredited investor looking at investing alongside us, we more than welcome you to see the knives we are catching.

Visit **CatchKnives.com** to learn more and find additional resources.

ACKNOWLEDGMENTS

There are so many things and people I feel blessed and incredibly grateful for. To acknowledge them all seems like quite a daunting task. So even though I feel like I could write a whole other book on thanking or acknowledging others who have helped this book come to fruition, I'll try to keep it under a hundred pages or so.

Of course, my beautiful, funny, smart, and amazing wife, Kristi, is without a doubt one of the best things that has ever happened to me. She has blessed me with a family, and honestly, my everyday life is already more than anything I had previously dreamed my life could become. She has changed my world, expanded my dreams, and helped me become a better man in all aspects of my life. With her by my side, I know we can go confidently in the direction of our dreams.

My mom, Margaret, is one of the most creative, smart, loving, selfless people I have ever met. I am also very biased because I think my mom is the best. I credit her with much of my vision and ability to think creatively. Most importantly, she gave me some sage advice that has stuck with me for many years. She told me to use my stubbornness to my benefit. Although it might have been difficult to parent a stubborn young Jake, she also had insight on how strong that determination was and how to harness that strength for good.

My dad, Michael, is one of the hardest working, funniest, and most skilled literary wordsmiths I have ever encountered. What I love about my dad, a retired police officer, is that he doesn't mince words and very much cuts straight to the point. When I was experiencing the subprime recession, he said something that stuck with me. He told me I didn't put in the work; I was always too smart for my own good and looking for the shortcut in life, and many times in life, you just have to put in the work. I have repeated that thought to myself many dozens of times when I questioned whether I was doing the work or looking for a shortcut.

Although those are a few of the main people who have had the biggest impacts on my life, that is not to belittle all the other people who have added value or made this book possible.

I have had many business partners, investors, friends, and family who have all been hugely helpful in making this book—and my career so far—what it has been.

Gabe: You have been my best friend my whole life, and as brothers, you have been through the ups and downs with me. You are one of the people I am most indebted to, and without your help, support, and love, I do not even know where I would be. Thank you for everything you have ever done.

Jason: Crazy how the world works. Your trust in me launched a whole new road of opportunity for me, and I hope that I can do the same for you. Thank you.

Anton: I feel blessed to have met you at the time I did. I feel like God opened the door to develop the business we did, and I am very blessed to call you a friend and partner.

GoBundance: This group of men has been one of those life-changing things for me. I found my tribe, and although I wish I found these brothers sooner, it is without a doubt one of the best things I have ever done.

There are so many other people I could thank but suffice to say that it has been a team effort to get where I am today.

God bless and good luck, you Contrarian Knife Catchers.

ABOUT THE
AUTHOR

JAKE HARRIS is the founder and managing partner of a private equity real estate firm that has managed, developed, and acquired more than $200 million in assets under management in the last five years alone. Jake has a master's degree in international real estate and is a licensed California broker and recognized expert in opportunity zones, infill development, construction cost-control systems, and the scaling of distressed investing business. To learn more about creating financial freedom through real estate investment, visit **www.catchknives.com**.